DEAD-END
DEMOCRACY?

Other fine books from the same publisher:

The Traitor and The Jew, by Esther Delisle
Zen & the Art of Post-Modern Canada, by Stephen Schecter
The Last Cod Fish, by Pol Chantraine
Seven Fateful Challenges for Canada, by Deborah Coyne
*A Canadian myth: Quebec, between Canada and the
Illusion of Utopia,* by William Johnson
Devil's Advocate, by Patrice Dutil
Economics in Crisis, by Louis-Philippe Rochon
Voltaire's Man in America, by Jean-Paul de Lagrave
Judaism: from the religious to the secular, by A.J. Arnold

Canadian Cataloguing in Publication Data

Leclerc, Yves, 1941-
  Dead-end democracy?
  Includes bibliographical references
  Translation of : La démocratie cul-de-sac.

  ISBN 1-895854-05-9
  1. Democracy.   2. International relations.   3. Civilization,
Western.   4. Intervention (International law).
I. Title

JC423.L4213 1994   321.8   C94-941252-X

This is the 6th book to appear in the Food for Thought series.

*If you would like to receive our current catalogue and
announcements of new titles, please send your name and address to:*
ROBERT DAVIES PUBLISHING,
P.O. Box 702, Outremont, Quebec, Canada H2V 4N6

Yves Leclerc

DEAD-END
DEMOCRACY?

translated by Madeleine Hébert,
with Jean-Paul Murray

Robert Davies Publishing
Montreal-Toronto

This book may be ordered in Canada from
General Distribution Services,
☎1-800-387-0141 / 1-800-387-0172 FAX 1-416-445-5967.
In the U.S.A., Toll-free 1-800-805-1083
Or from the publisher, (514)481-2440,FAX (514)481-9973.

Original title:
La Démocratie cul-de-sac (l'Étincelle éditeur, 1993)

The publisher takes this opportunity to thank the
Canada Council and the *Ministère de la Culture du Québec*
for their continuing support.

Cover illustration :
interpreted detail of *Carnavales* by Rene Portocarrero

To Marie-José, my first reader...
and my first critic!

TABLE OF CONTENTS

Introduction
DEAD-END DEMOCRACY?

D emocracy is a defective product. Needs a recall. And yet, like the proverbial used-car salesman, we obstinately continue peddling it to the rest of the world in its present, dubious form. Behind the propaganda barrage promoting the "democratic ideal" and commercial liberalism, lies in fact our attempt to impose our own ideological, economic and political views on the rest of mankind, who are, to put it mildly, tired of our pounding sloganeering: "Democracy is progress," "no justice without democracy," or "democracy is a precondition to any international aid," which is even more tendentious, since it implies a kind of development blackmail.

For some time, Americans and their European allies have, in the name of this ideal, arrogated to themselves the right to use military or economic force in the affairs of other states, with or without the United Nations' acquiescence. They might justify this on the basis of a quasi-universal consensus, if it was done coherently and equitably. But the appearance of a consensus is only exacted through intense social and political pressure; intervention is seemingly a function of friendships or enmities or, simpler yet, the narrow interests of one or the other, not to mention a certain degree of racism. The indecent haste in Iraq and the even more obscene delay in the former Yugoslavia are recent examples of both extremes.

Yet, we talk and act as though certain we've devised, in a half-dozen generations, the ultimate solution to problems affecting societies for at least five millennia. We seem to believe political and social evolution should suddenly culminate with a formula discovered only recently in our little corner of the world—and greatly tinkered with since. It's as though we wanted to adopt the Nazi catch phrase of an "empire lasting a thousand years," a formula extensively and justifiably decried.

The promotion of the democratic concept has gradually ceased to be a matter of logic; it's become a kind of religious belief. And, like most religions, it exudes the stale smell of magic ... and intolerance. Anybody questioning the slightest iota is looked on like the heretic or heathen of old. On the other hand, those who preach it have the same paternalistic and rather spiteful attitude that crusaders and conquistadors had towards " infidels." For them, the systematic application of the recipe will inevitably yield beneficial results, regardless of specific circumstances or the logic of a situation ... which is precisely the definition of magic. Their direct rivals, the Islamic fundamentalists, are no better in this regard.

This attitude had particularly perverse effects recently in Eastern Europe, Somalia and Cambodia. It's still at work in much of the Third World where, against common sense, efforts are made to establish bourgeois democracy, i.e., by relying on aristocratic elites and a population that's frequently illiterate, in the absence of the system's cornerstone, the middle class. This despite increasingly conclusive evidence that economic progress, where resources are scarce, can only be achieved under authoritarian regimes, able to impose long-term strategies and make difficult and unpopular decisions, preferably in the absence of electoral constraints.

A virtual high-pressure sale of democracy has been taking place for nearly a half century; yet, the sociopolitical model it proposes is far from keeping all its promises. Few of the hundred or so new countries born from decolonization have freely adopted, or long maintained, this formula. Those that did are not visibly wealthier, more stable, or even more just than others that achieved independence at the same time, favoring oligarchic or outright dictatorial regimes.

Many states among those that invented or advocate it are at grips with social and economic problems that democracy can't solve ... when it isn't itself partly the cause. Signs of a widespread illness are multiplying. In 1992 alone, the following occurred: the Los Angeles riots, and the popularity surge of billionaire Ross Perot as a "third candidate" from outside the party framework in the U.S. election campaign; the rise of the " Front national " and the near rejection of the Maastricht treaty in France; urban problems and other difficulties for the Major government in the United Kingdom; the NO to constitutional reform (and by extension to the political, intellectual, labor and financial elites) in Canada; the rise of neo-Nazism in a reunified Germany; the return to power of communists in Lithuania; the disintegration of the USSR and of Yugoslavia (Which some have had the temerity to call a "democratization"), etc.

I've long believed, like most, that such crises were random mishaps, having little to do with our form of government, the only one imaginable for a modern state. Until the angry comment of a Tukolor chief from Kaolack, which I'd heard three or four years ago in Senegal, came back to mind and inspired me to look at the question from another angle. "Your white man's democracy," he'd said, "is worthless. What reasonable man can accept as equally valid the opinion of a twenty-year old kid who thinks only of chasing girls, and that of a sixty-year old man who has the experience of a lifetime?"

This seemingly whimsical rejoinder convincingly refutes a fundamental premise of Western-style democracy: one man, one vote—regardless of the man or the vote's purpose. It condemns our system on the basis of a cultural consideration, i.e., the assumption that wisdom is a function of maturity. This notion isn't only African; it's shared by numerous societies on at least three continents. Therefore, it can't be dismissed by an "ad hominem" argument such as "Who are the Africans to give us lessons on government?" at the risk of being answered "But who are Westerners to lecture the rest of mankind?"

The democracy we advocate began in a very specific context: the Protestant (or deist) European world at the beginning of the industrial age. Other cultures and traditions have different ideas about power and the demands of government, which it would be pretentious to call primitive. In China, at least sixty generations of public service have ensured that the only way of reaching a position of civil authority is following an adequate education and a battery of exams confirming competence: forty-odd years of socialism—excluding the "cultural revolution," which ran against the grain—haven't disproved this view in the least. For nearly a quarter of mankind, then, taking power by winning a popularity contest, with no previous guarantee of competence (the true nature of a modern election when stripped of its ersatz philosophical facade), likely seems absurd, even dangerous.

Better yet, when Churchill, somewhat tongue-in-cheek, said, "democracy is the worst form of government except all those other forms that have been tried," he spoke from a Judaeo-Christian perspective; his judgment was leveled at the substance rather than the form or cultural context. Interestingly, the denunciation contained in the first part of the phrase was quickly forgotten and only the second part retained; an authoritative argument, justifying the transformation into an absolute ideal of the relative and rather ambiguous concept of "government by the people," has been drawn from this reluctant admission.

However, if democracy really is flawed, as Churchill said, then it deserves to be opposed, or at least submitted to rigorous analysis, either to replace it with something better (if possible), or at least to identify and minimize its adverse effects. Although there's a tendency to ignore these or blame them on other factors, they're common and injurious. Nevertheless, open attacks against the system have been rare over the last century, usually in the guise of modest attempts to remedy such effects. The absence of a serious critical examination nurtured by public debate has meant that these efforts have mostly failed.

In essence, we maintain that problems with democracy are temporary, or the result of defective usage, and that its underpinnings are sound. The time has come to ask whether, on the contrary, the system carries the seeds of its failures, and whether the concept itself is flawed. This question isn't new: over two thousand years ago, Pericles and Aristotle questioned the popular election of rulers as a means of ensuring competent and honest government. But it's been completely ignored in the great and blind rush to impose our views to the world.

Hence, this book. Does it really take an opposing view of democracy, as its title suggests? Yes, since it aims at systematically highlighting its defects and inconsistencies, without worrying about putting a positive gloss on the analysis. Yes, because it seeks to demolish what we've made of it—an unquestionable ideal—and restore its true nature, that of a shaky compromise certainly open to debate. And yes, finally, given the term as used by its oracles doesn't refer to the philosophical precept that power comes from the people, to whom those exercising it are accountable, but rather, to *an elitist system that exploits the people's will without respecting it*. In this sense, democracy really is a dead-end we must try to escape. The situation is comparable to that of Europe in the days of Martin Luther: although he remained a Christian, Luther saw that the Catholic church had become so corrupt and wandered so far from its original principles, that he had to fight it head on, instead of reforming it from within.

If this book vigorously criticizes "democracy," it's not for the self-indulgent pleasure of doing so, nor to foolishly go back in history to revive systems that are even more unjust and ineffective. I'm neither a monarchist, nor a fascist, and remain convinced that a community of men can only be properly governed with their consent. However, I'll make no efforts to "balance" the picture by underlining the obvious qualities and advantages of the democratic system; others have done this exhaustively ... without mentioning the weaknesses I intend to stress.

My perspective isn't that of a politician or lawyer, but that of an ordinary citizen who's observed a lot, is reasonably well-read and has pondered somewhat. A citizen who, because of his profession as a journalist, has occasionally been at the front lines and seen the mechanisms of power turn at full throttle and then seize up under the weight of rapid change, social tensions and internal contradictions. Add to that the vicissitudes of life, which later led me to examine the same events thoroughly, from the perspective of the unemployed (the quasi-outlaws, or pariahs in our society) compelled to reduce the problems of civilization to the level of basic needs. The level referred to by a Haitian friend who, returning from a trip at the time when President Aristide was ousted, answered my volley of questions on the situation in his country as follows: "Today in Haiti, my friend, the only real question is 'Ki maniè ou ka cuit'ça, Démokrasi?'" or, in other words, what's the recipe for cooking democracy: we're dying of hunger?

A word on the method I've chosen, which may baffle some readers. It's neither an elaborate accumulation of facts, often favored by fellow journalists, nor quotations and authoritative arguments proper to academics. It's rather an enquiry attempting to be rational and rigorous, supported by facts that are often conflicting, not to impress or scandalize, but to seek out a certain logical order. I'm specifically striving—despite difficulties and not always with total success—to avoid the white-European ethnocentrism which too often earmarks this sort of endeavor. The techniques are those I've learned over fifteen years of scientific and technological popularization, applied to a completely different domain, that of political ideas and realities: return to original sources, simplification of ideas and elimination of obviously irrelevant details, comparison of diverging opinions, grouping of facts into concrete and comprehensible categories, translation of abstract and esoteric vocabulary into more familiar and meaningful terms, application of common-sense principles.

My goal is to provide a wide canvas, using broad brush strokes, that's coherent and proportional to the knowledge of a reader who is intelligent but not always be well-informed. My aim isn't to prove a thesis, but to dismantle a mechanism and expose its workings ... to better illustrate the reasons for its chronic failures. If, so doing, I happen to discover evidence that runs counter to "conventional wisdom" more often than anticipated, it's a pure (and to my thinking, a happy) coincidence.

I've also wagered on brevity and clarity; to achieve this, I've abstained from parading all authors consulted, or mentioning all the examples, statistics and historical references, and exhausting all research sources. The resulting document may seem impressionistic; but this matters little to me, as long as the reasoning is sound and buttressed by sufficient concrete material. This possibility might even please me: the incomplete and suggestive nature of the work should urge the reader to pursue the inquiry in directions I've overlooked. Should that happen, and lead to results that surprise or even contradict me, I'll deem myself successful.

Have I chosen a deliberately provocative title? Certainly. This is a proven literary and intellectual device; I'll only mention Erasmus and Zola among many illustrious predecessors. The alternative would have been to provide a more discreet title, such as "A Critique of the Anglo-Franco-American Democratic Model;" it would then have reached only professional thinkers and political science enthusiasts. But I believe the problem concerns all those living in what we call democracies ... or in the far more numerous undemocratic regimes we are trying to convert. This book is directed to them, in the somewhat Quixotic hope of briefly halting that enormous, infernal machine hurling us blindly towards a "new world order." A condition that remains highly questionable and one I doubt will make the planet more livable for the majority of mankind.

_1_

A QUESTIONABLE IDEAL

Democracy is willingly depicted as an ancient, proven and universal system, profoundly rooted in our customs. A wonderful gift to mankind from the West, which owes its well-being and superiority to it. An ideal, therefore, beyond suspicion and criticism. This fiction we mistake for reality rests on a double falsehood or, at the very least, a double misunderstanding.

First, there's confusion about the word. When our leaders and thinkers praise "democracy" and insist on the importance of spreading its benefits to the entire planet, they lead us to believe they're referring to a generally applicable philosophico-political doctrine we inherited from ancient Greece and define, in Lincoln's words, as "government of the people, by the people, for the people." What they're really talking about is a very specific type of system that doesn't nearly respect all the doctrine's principles, but grafts to it ideas with which it has no fundamental link.

For example, power isn't exercised by the people, but by representatives given a mandate the electorate can't rescind prematurely; it isn't necessarily exercised for the people, since leaders aren't held to the promises they made to get elected (a Canadian Supreme Court judgment confirms this outright). On the other hand, our system mandatorily presupposes a capitalist economy and the primacy of individual over collective rights, two concepts foreign to the theory: in the past, systems completely democratic in spirit and structure may have been, or were, communist and totalitarian (for example, Thomas More's Utopia or the Athens of Pericles).

In fact, what we call democracy, as emphasized at the turn of the century by Hans Kelsen and Robert Michels, is really a liberal system—both socially and economically—of the electoral type having oligarchical leanings. That is, a system based on the concept of individual freedom, using an electoral mechanism to maintain an insular "political class" essentially spawned from the affluent middle class and renewed through co-optation. That class usually gets the upper hand in any showdown with the people, if only because it's united. Recent examples of this phenomenon, which Michels calls "the iron law of oligarchy," are too numerous to mention.

Second, the historical perspective is distorted. Without going into detail, it's easy to demonstrate that democracy is a recent form of government, even where it originated. Its shape is still far from definite; its philosophical underpinnings clearly bear the mark of very specific social, cultural, religious and economic circumstances; its alleged benefits generally existed before it appeared; and its implementation occurred unevenly, often brutally, accompanied by jolts, resistance and frequent backsliding. It is, at the very least a questionable ideal.

A RECENT INVENTION

First, despite the claims of its promoters, democracy is an invention, or better, a modern reinvention having little in common with the ancient forms of government to which it claims lineage and which carried the same name in Greece or Rome. For instance, the Athenian formula was aristocratic and, for a good part of its history, non-elective. In peacetime, most of its leaders were chosen by drawing lots (some for only a day, none for more than a year) among citizens recognized by their peers as "worthy;" in wartime, the choice was made by consensus, according to merit and experience. Important decisions were made following public discussions involving all citizens; political parties were considered highly suspect. Although the Roman Republic, for its part, was elective, it greatly limited the duration and scope of mandates. Its assembly mechanisms and distribution of public office divided society basically into hereditary classes and castes, the mere mention of which would offend our egalitarian sensibilities.

These two examples confirm that extremely different systems can hide behind the same label and that the shape of ours has nothing absolute or inevitable. For example, the goal of ancient systems was to prevent an oligarchy from seizing and maintaining power; ours has the opposite effect, at least, if not the objective. It cannot therefore claim direct lineage to these predecessors; it can, at the outside and very indirectly, trace its origins to medieval "free cities" or communes. Most of these had a brief and precarious existence and their government structures were empirical, without the least ideological basis.

The foundations of our democracy were laid by a few 16th and 17th century forerunners, whose influence in their time was marginal, given the predominance of divine-right monarchies fully supported by the Church. As well, most of these shrank from advocating direct popular sovereignty. Erasmus, Jean Bodin, Hugo Grotius and Thomas Hobbes were preoccupied with ideas such as the impartiality and continuity of the law and the legitimacy of authority, but generally considered as "natural" the monarchical mechanism for transferring power by heredity. Machiavelli, although a devout republican, is much better known for his dissection of absolute power, while Thomas More, an ardent Christian, was a fervent communist before the term existed. The concept of power belonging by right to the people—if an insular class of owners and shopkeepers can be considered as the people—and the obligation of rulers to be publicly accountable for their mandates, only clearly emerged with John Locke, Jean-Jacques Rousseau and Thomas Jefferson.

Democracy offered a realistic political alternative only at the very end of the 18th century in France and in the rebellious British North American colonies. Interestingly, the system that served as a model for its inventors, sometimes positively, sometimes negatively, is the British monarchy. During a lengthy struggle for power, first between the crown and nobles ("Magna Carta," 1215), then between the latter and the bourgeoisie (Cromwell, 1648-1659), it developed customary rules and institutions—elected Parliament, "habeas corpus," division of power—that fascinated and inspired French democrats. On the other hand, the Americans, who endured the monarchy as colonial subjects, mistrusted it and designed political mechanisms to avoid or correct its injustices and oppressiveness. It was to protect the people against the exactions of an absolute royal power that Jefferson, Franklin and their companions devised the first Bill of Rights and the doctrine of individual rights as fundamental values.

As well, it was no accident that democracy appeared where and when it did. A little over two centuries ago, North-Central Europe (consisting entirely of monarchies, save for Switzerland) simultaneously underwent a sharp decrease in the Catholic clergy's power, a sudden surge in the influence of the financial and merchant class, the dawn of the capitalist industrial age and an unprecedented period of prosperity. All this was favored, if not caused, by the massive exploitation of colonial resources, and particularly with a workforce that was poorly paid, if at all, provided by the slave trade and forced child labor. All these "advantages" preceded democracy and were in no way caused by it.

As far as we can judge from European and American experience, the system is a luxury available only to societies already enjoying a certain affluence. Ultimately, we can imagine the West wouldn't have become democratic, had it not been a colonial slavocracy ... and only a hint of bad faith is required to maintain that any culture wanting the same results needs only follow the same path!

All our theoreticians of the system, whether French, English or American, were male, Protestant (or deist like Voltaire) and bourgeois (or maverick aristocrats like Condorcet). The model they proposed aimed, under the guise of universality, to resolve problems very specific to their time, and notably to pave the way to political power for the industrial and merchant class already dominating the economy. Most of these "fathers of democracy" remained explicitly or implicitly favorable to slavery, sought to limit voting rights to the elite and propertied classes, and vigorously opposed any political status for women.

A CHAOTIC EVOLUTION

Evolving gradually, their style of democracy spread to European countries only slowly and painfully in the following century and a half. Even today, England, Spain, Norway, Belgium, the Netherlands, and a few others, remain monarchies on the surface at least. While France is at its fifth incarnation of the republican formula, Germany and Italy are at their first or second genuine attempts. In fact, a parliamentary system that recognizes the equality of most citizens has existed for more than a century only in North America, Switzerland and, with the notable constraint that the crown has been maintained, in the United Kingdom.

As well, until the 1950s, Western countries adhering to democracy took care not to spread its benefits to their colonies, except when compelled ... and usually on condition power be held by European descendants. The few non-white states that attempted the experiment (Haiti, Liberia) were submitted to a more or less discreet ostracism, helping them remain among the poorest regions of the world and, in the long run, throwing them into the arms of dictatorship.

Even between the two world wars, authentic European democracies could still be counted on the fingers of one hand and their life expectancy was very brief. Many of those countries violently repudiated "government by the people" because of social or economic crises, replacing them with totalitarian systems: nazism, fascism, falangism are, as much as liberal democracy, Western political "discoveries." Moreover, the reaction they elicited in their still-recent time was at least one of sympathetic curiosity, if not outright enthusiasm.

Meanwhile, the Soviet Union's experience, and that of its satellites and imitators, seemed to offer a credible alternative in the form of a single-party and communist "popular republic." This solution confronted liberalism with a radically different principle, the dictatorship of the proletariat which seduced as many new independent countries as our democracy. I'm not attempting to vindicate communism (that would be rather inappropriate in the present context), but only to underline that the level of mutual criticism guaranteed by the East-West ideological rivalry and the frequent indifference to democratic evangelism by the "free world," which accommodated itself rather well with other regimes, as long as they were anticommunist, curtailed the need to question the democratic principle.

The situation has changed dramatically in a very short time: the collapse of the USSR and socialist states in Europe was widely interpreted as the triumph and vindication of the Anglo-Franco-American political and ideological model. At the same time, the aggressive clarion call of our neighbor to the south, the only superpower left, now exclusive master of the territory of the propaganda of historical "success", again raises the question in all its intensity and with added urgency: is democracy, in itself and as we practise it, a solution so evident and so perfect that we have the right to impose it on the rest of the world, through a combination of enticements and threats?

THE ERROR OF MEN

I'm far from the only one to have raised this question. Critical essays on various aspects of this theme have abounded over the last few years. Although many of these dissertations were written in a scholarly style requiring a political culture way beyond the average citizen's, most of their authors limited themselves to an analytical level that seems dangerously superficial to me. They posit as a basic hypothesis that the system isn't defective; it's the context that creates deviations (ironically, that was also Gorbachev's view of the problems of the Soviet system). More specifically, they denounce the ignorance and volatility of the electorate, the complacency and maliciousness of the media and the resulting dubious choice of leaders.

If we were to believe them, it's not the system that's corrupt, but those who operate it. For various reasons arising from uncontrollable and pernicious circumstances, we have too frequently permitted the election (by accident or fraud) of governments whose wickedness, stupidity and incompetence are responsible for the present mess. One of the most ambitious and convincing endeavors in this regard is probably that of Guy Hermet in "Le peuple contre la démocratie" (Fayard, 1989).

A list of human blunders—at least a partial one—is easy to draw up for the last two decades. There was Richard Nixon's wallowing in Watergate intrigue, Giscard d'Estaing's chumminess with the diamond-rich Emperor Bokassa of the Central African Republic, Willy Brandt's social-democratic government suffering from acute spy mania, a great deal of nasty business combining sex, indiscretions and money before and during the Thatcher regime in the United Kingdom, the strange weapons-money-hostages swap of the Irangate where Ronald Reagan was represented by his vice-president and successor, George Bush, the impeachment of Fernando Collor de Melo, caught red-handed in Brazil, the flirt with dictatorship by Alberto Fujimori, Peru's disquieting but fascinating president, the prolonged and secretive courtship of Bettino Craxi, and many other Italian politicians, with the Mafia (criminal and financial) … Need I continue?

In human societies, bashing politicians is a completely natural and instinctive reaction. When something goes awry, we seek the guilty party or parties. In the present case, they're easy to find, since shady, incompetent and short-sighted leaders are aplenty. They may be no more numerous in the political arena than elsewhere, but their visibility makes them easier targets. Pointing to them with indignation and exposing them to public condemnation allows us to evade the more fundamental and disturbing questions, of which the first should be: "if our system is so perfect, why are such characters carried to power so often?"

FAULTY IMPLEMENTATION

Given the persistence and pervasiveness of these problems, and especially the new impossibility of blaming "Godless communists," we finally understand that pillorying guilty parties is at best inadequate and, in many cases, simply unjust. Many political thinkers have therefore pushed their reasoning to the point of admitting that the democratic formula we apply (with variations that are sometimes considerable from one country to the other) is not flawless, and remains on many levels remote from its theoretical model; this second level of criticism began nearly a century ago with authors like Michels, Pareto and Mosca, but has gained much importance in the last fifteen years.

To deal with practical flaws, we've either resignedly accepted them as neutral "characteristics," if not advantages, or we've chosen to pursue two somewhat contradictory approaches to correct them. One of the best examples of the first view is the German economist Joseph Schumpeter (who ended his career in the U.S. as a Harvard professor); following a brilliant and merciless critique of the system's classical theory in "Capitalism, Socialism and Democracy," he concludes that, all things considered, democracy has nothing to do with government by the people; it's simply a formula for competitive access to power within a restricted political elite—a mission it accomplishes very well!

The two "corrective" approaches mentioned are far from mutually exclusive: many countries have tried them individually or jointly. The first, with claims to populism, is an attempt to re-establish the democratic concept's original purity through a kind of return to the source. The second, which takes on airs of modernity, seeks instead to adapt political and electoral mechanisms to new realities that didn't exist when the theory was conceived.

The propositions emanating from the first approach contain three main ideas: extending the democratic process upwards, increasing the representativity of proceedings, and requiring the population to specifically apprise leaders about their preferences. The first idea favors the direct participation of citizens, not only in the choice of elected members, but in that of candidates as well (primaries and caucuses in the U.S., voting by all party members, not only delegates, at nomination meetings in many countries); the second tries to establish a better correlation between the composition of decision-making assemblies and that of the population (quotas for women, youth, minorities); the last one elicits direct public participation in decisions through referenda, thereby at least partly correcting the oligarchic tendency.

Unfortunately, we often observe with astonished indignation that these remedies aggravate, rather than cure, the ailments. Candidates chosen by the people lack the minimum competence required, the legislation adopted unduly and haphazardly favors or disadvantages a particular segment of society, according to temporary alliances between pressure groups, public consultations go against the opinions of leaders, who are forced to give in to tendencies they feel are absurd or suicidal. When all else fails, we rely on "adjustments" that, paradoxically tend to be even less democratic: referenda are considered "indicative" and not binding, a supreme court appointed by the executive obtains the power to overthrow a law adopted by the people's representatives, candidacies are more or less secretly screened beforehand to ensure a minimum of experience and honesty ...

The second approach seeks to eliminate the deviant effects of certain recent phenomena, most of them having a scientific or technological origin:

- the electronic media's dominant influence on public opinion, its emphasis on form over substance, and its compression of ideas into instant "bytes," as striking as they are simplistic;
- refined techniques for marketing men and slogans that transform all campaigns into image and propaganda battles, rather than debates of ideas;
- the rise of polls and other statistical tools whose results, even if valid, lead to unscrupulous use and whose impact on public opinion and on government style is undeniable, though difficult to quantify.

However, since we consider democracy as a sacred cow whose least tuft of hair cannot be tousled (at least openly), proposed "corrections" are limited to damage control. They reduce or circumvent the drawbacks of these innovations, without the least effort to adapt their possible advantages into the system. For instance, try to suggest that polls should have a positive and recognized role in the process, or that " on-screen government " as exercised on television by more and more heads of state, should be standardized and regulated. You'll cause an immediate public protest, without anybody bothering to weigh the soundness of such propositions.

A CULTURAL REJECTION

A third type of criticism has been raised by Third-World leaders and political scientists, and is beginning to emerge among Western authors. It begins with the observation that, if democracy has taken solid root in Europe and in regions of America mostly populated by European descendants (even then, that claim is strongly challenged by recent events in the former Soviet Bloc and by Latin America's entire history), this isn't so in the rest of the world.

Very few states created since 1950, either from decolonization or the partition of existing nations, are democracies;

those that are, are neither wealthier nor more peaceful than the average.

Some—like Singapore and Senegal—have assumed the reassuring facade of an elected parliament, while actually functioning in very tight circles, like oligarchies. A strong majority openly adopted different regimes: absolute monarchy, theocracy, civilian or military dictatorship, people's republic. In many cases, they reached that condition following brief and disastrous attempts at democratic government.

We may therefore rightly ask whether Western-style democracy is an exportable commodity, or whether it's so saturated with the thought and social structure of Northern Europe and America that it automatically produces a "cultural-rejection" syndrome as soon as we try to graft it to other cultures. Our thinkers' usual response, that non-Europeans "are too backwards" to clearly perceive democracy's benefits, and that they only need to be educated, doesn't stand up to analysis: some of those societies had governments capable of administering empires when our ancestors were still hunting boar in Central European forests—remember that Montesquieu marveled that separation of power had appeared "in the woods"—and cities where a majority of the population could read and write, at a time when our illiterate kings had to have their edicts spelled out for them by those rare monks who could do so. Whether those peoples used Parsee or Arabic symbols or ideograms, instead of the Latin alphabet, changes nothing ... it only underlines the latent racism of many of our "progressive" thinkers.

The other solution we're beginning to contemplate, that the formula itself lacks universality, has the double merit of insulting no one and being more accurate. It's notably the one which explains most plainly the sporadic emergence on other continents of somewhat eccentric leaders pretending to seek indigenous avenues towards democracy or, more generally, an equitable political system that respects the needs and desires of its peoples. They're viewed with sympathy and encouraged by the "great powers," wherever the formulas they concocted take hold smoothly, under relatively conservative administrations, and maintain a superficial resemblance with what we know. In other cases, they are condemned as undemocratic, even before having a chance to provide results, and are destabilized by methods bearing the earmarks of the finest imperialism.

We can understand the system's inventors would have believed, a century or two ago, that what seemed to apply to Europeans was by definition universal. First, they lacked modern knowledge about other cultures. Moreover, they viewed the rest of the world through the eyes of colonizers, for whom whatever didn't resemble them was either savage or primitive. Finally, they had the perennial flaw, which we haven't nearly eradicated, of believing that their time and corner of the world represented the height of civilization. Their mistakes may therefore be forgiven. What cannot, is that we continue to lay claim to universality on the shaky foundations they established.

Two flagrant examples of this cultural myopia are private property and the party system, two of the allegedly universal foundations of the structure. In the first case, all reasoning since John Locke rests on the "natural" and instinctive necessity of carving territory into individual properties. This model likely prevailed in Europe due to limited space and population growth; it was transplanted as such in "white" colonies. But it's foreign to nearly all indigenous American societies, throughout most of the Arab world, in the Black-African interior, in the Asian steppes (nomadic populations) and in Oceania, where land either belonged to no one or to everybody. Clearly, a definition of property (and by extension of freedom) based on this "principle" must seem absurd to all those peoples.

As for party structure, it presupposes a division into social classes and a certain ethnic and religious homogeneity in the population, characteristics that correspond to nothing wherever, for example, there exists a system of socio-religious castes or a tribal structure based on ethnic differences. In those areas, parties created in the name of democracy will either correspond directly to castes and tribes, thus reinforcing differences, or be artificially grafted on communities where they'll only add to confusion. In both cases, it's difficult to see how they might play an effective role in the government mechanism and deliver the benefits they promise.

A recent book, Bertrand Badie's "L'État importé: l'occidentalisation de l'ordre politique" (Fayard, 1993), exposes this level of criticism in a very articulate though somewhat arid manner. Badie emphasizes that, in reality, both democracy and its socialist rival are European cultural products; he places much of the blame on local elites, whom he believes are unable to make the necessary adjustments—but he doesn't sufficiently underscore that these elites are often too europeanized, too cut-off from their own roots to achieve a transformation that is perhaps completely impossible.

MORE FUNDAMENTAL FLAWS

I flatly reject the first type of analysis mentioned above: pretending that social crises are caused by "human error" distorts the problem and prevents an understanding of the forces at play; obviously, any workable political system must effectively consider the uncertainties of human nature and can't therefore use them as alibis. On the other hand, I believe the two other levels of criticism (deviation from the model and cultural differences) rest on solid foundations. In fact, I'll frequently resort to them in the following pages. But are they sufficient? In my opinion, no. They don't go to the root of the problem and it would be a serious mistake to limit ourselves to them.

That's why the main part of my argument lies elsewhere, in a fourth and more fundamental level of analysis, where almost no one dares venture today, likely from fear of being accused of "lèse-liberalism." The question that troubles me is the following: *does the democratic system work, even assuming honest governments elected according to the rules, even with an improved and modernized political design, and even in a favorable political context?* Or, does it not instead have inherent and somewhat hidden flaws, structural and operational defects that make it, in Churchill's words "the worst system?" Among its most obvious imperfections are the three following:

a) A poor method for choosing leaders.

b) The impossibility of long-term planning.

c) The inevitable emergence of a society in perpetual conflict.

Most of what follows is dedicated to this question. Accordingy, we'll examine the nature of the "social contract" that supposedly binds a nation and its leaders, the persistent conflict between "respect for individual freedoms" and "defence of public interest," problems with long-term planning (and adjusting the aim in the short term) in an electoral context and finally, the adversarial but very powerful links between liberal democracy and capitalism. Where will this study lead? Those expecting a comprehensive and immediately applicable solution from such a brief overview will be disappointed; my goal isn't to clutter the horizon with another ready-made formula, but to open it to new levels of reflection and discussion. As mentioned in the introduction, my approach is that of a technical popularizer, not an ideologue. I'll limit myself to dismantling the mechanism and explaining why it works so poorly. To conclude, I'll raise a few hypotheses and provide a number of leads suggested by common logic and a non-doctrinal view of circumstances, that are likely to propel us, gradually or abruptly, peacefully or violently, "beyond democracy."

-2-

THE SOCIAL-CONTRACT COMPROMISE

To explain the nature of the state and that of politics, we frequently devise grand theories, appeal to authoritative arguments, and perform meticulous dissections of techniques and procedures. These approaches no doubt suit the needs of power practitioners and authors wishing to enlighten and advise them.

They aren't suitable in this case, however, since my approach is completely different: I'm addressing all citizens of so-called democratic countries and those we're attempting to convert. The best means of understanding the main points of such an arcane subject is to begin with the simplest facts, by observing societies at various stages of their development, and proceed by stages to more general conclusions. Fortunately, there exist today practical examples of nearly all the evolutional stages of nations, from the tiny cave-dwelling tribes of Borneo or the Philippines, to the supranational complexity of the European Community, through African tribal structures, the nomadic patriarchate of certain Arab peoples, the feudalism of many oriental states, Canadian or German federalism and the Iranian theocracy. There's obviously no shortage of raw material.

Let's start by agreeing on definitions. Many terms are used indiscriminately to designate political phenomena; however, in the context of this study, it's useful to single out their subtleties and agree on their meaning.

PEOPLE: A group of individuals living on the same territory or having a common culture, customs and system of government.

SOCIETY: The condition of people living in an organized association. Individuals bound by a culture, institutions, etc.

NATION: A human community defined as a political entity, living on a territory or a group of specific territories and constitutionally organized as a state.

STATE: A legal entity personifying the nation inside and outside the country it governs.

GOVERNMENT: The power governing the state.

According to these definitions (simply drawn from the dictionary), there's a certain overlap among the words people, society and nation. All refer to the human community but distinctions can be made: the first places emphasis on the body of citizens, the second on social and cultural links, the third on the political aspect. On the other hand, the definitions of state and government are more specific: one is a legal entity representing the community's sovereignty, the other is its administrative apparatus.

In practice, if we rely on these definitions, society is not a political entity, even if its evolution has important political repercussions. The people may be divided, but the nation is always indivisible. An important and unforeseen consequence of this distinction: if politicians represent the nation, they must take orders from it. If they represent the people, they must govern according to their own judgment, without being forced to respect various public opinion trends. We'll see further on that this difference has important practical effects.

We can also claim that public interest and sovereign political powers belong to the nation, but are administered or exercised by the state, which includes the legislature (houses of representatives and senates), the executive and administrative branches (the government), the judiciary (the courts), and I'm tempted to add an information branch (the press). The status of the press is only officially recognized in the U.S., albeit indirectly; this situation ought to improve as other developed countries increasingly understand the role of information.

The vocabulary problem being solved, the first question concerns the "social contract," that explicit agreement between leaders and citizens that sets the rules of the game, as it were, and lays the foundation of democracy. Among the "inventors" of our system, Hobbes and Rousseau uphold the principle, whereas Montesquieu and Bentham don't see its necessity. Do we really need it to explain the advent of politics?

Plain observation indicates a contract isn't necessary to create a human society, as long as it isn't structured. In fact, man is a gregarious animal naturally inclined to group living (extended family, tribe, village), without there being a conscious volition or explicit agreement; similarly, ants, deer and wolves live in colonies, herds or packs without agreement to do so. Human defence and reproductive mechanisms alone mean that survival beyond one or two generations would be extremely difficult for the isolated individual or even the biological family.

Therefore, contrary to what Hobbes believed, sociability must be part of the species' genetic baggage. This implies that, despite what nineteenth century "utilitarians" and their liberal direct descendants tried to prove, humans must possess an innate sense of collective responsibility that differs from an aggregate of individual interests. A clue to its existence is that most heroes throughout history became prominent not for their individualism or egotism but, on the contrary, for having behaved and often sacrificed themselves for the community. This theme is too pervasive throughout human cultures to be dismissed as purely accidental.

A POLITICAL COMPACT

The second phase consists in rationalizing group life; it may appear very quickly, much later, or never. Once the community has grown, it must be organized and governed; at that stage, it becomes a society and discovers power. In other words, we don't have to imagine a "double contract" as do some philosophers, since its first component, which causes creation of the group, is instinctive and shared by various animal species. But, while community organization is part of the genetic code for these species, that isn't the case for humans (even at the family level, which can be patriarchal or matriarchal, nuclear or extended): it varies according to circumstances and customs, which suggests that it results from a more or less explicit and desired agreement.

This second component, which is specific to man and therefore concerns us, is the political contract. In its most primitive form, group members chose or submit themselves to a leader and define or let him define the extent of his power. The latter case is a tyranny in the technical sense, i.e., without the pejorative overtones given to it by everyday language; the former usually witnesses the creation of checks against possible excesses: a senate, popular assembly, electoral system, feudal structure...

In the beginning, division of power likely didn't exist: the executive, legislative and judiciary were held in the same hands and answered to the same rules. There quickly emerged, however, a distinction that was sometimes rudimentary. There were leaders responsible for peace, others for war, an executive handled public works and tax collecting, the law was established by custom or edict (and often ratified by elders), religious or secular judges settled disagreements, the police gradually detached itself from the army. This division of tasks was a harbinger to separation of powers, which is a much more modern invention.

Careful scrutiny will no doubt reveal exceptions to this process, but everything I've seen in daily life and read by historians and ethnologists indicates it's a universal rule. Its existence is neither surprising, nor miraculous: it responds to a series of needs common to all men that only collective living can satisfy on a durable basis: subsistence, shelter, reproduction, security. When Marx described man as a "complex of needs," he largely thought in economic terms; but the structural needs of reproduction (registry office) and security (judicial apparatus and military complex) which underpin many of political society's powers, are just as real and likely as important.

Some will be offended that the need for freedom isn't on the list. But as far as I know, it's a consequence rather than a prerequisite. It's hard to imagine calls for freedom preceding oppression; in fact, slavery is a social and economic relation that is too pervasive in the history of human societies on all continents for freedom to be posited as an instinctive or "natural" need. For this reason, it can't be considered as a stipulation of the primitive compact.

Ever since John Locke claimed that the principal purpose for creating civil society is the preservation of property, the right to property—ownership of land primarily—has been one of the "basic needs" favored by liberals. Trouble is, many societies never knew property in general, or ownership of land in particular. The latter only could have appeared when societies settled permanently and became agricultural; even then, the occurrence is far from universal. For example, in the case of certain North-American aboriginal tribes, the land cultivated was commonly owned; even women and children belonged to the entire community. Therefore, that need couldn't have been part of the original pact either.

Here's another interesting observation: in primitive societies the family is the basic unit of political organization, not the individual. The isolated man has no status; he's only accepted by the group if he joins a family through adoption or marriage. The inclusion of unattached individuals into society likely occurred much later, following the emergence of definite political structures, and to widely varying degrees from one culture to the other—the family as keystone of the State is an idea that was still found among thinkers such as Bodin and Althusius in pre-democratic 16th century Europe.

An important conclusion arises from the three previous paragraphs: we can't claim the theoretical foundations of liberal democracy as we know it ("one man, one vote" as political mechanism, property as economic mainspring, and individual freedom as legal foundation) to be natural. They don't arise logically from the social contract either, whatever their ethical or practical merits.

NATURE OF THE CONTRACT

In the form we believe it exists, the "social contract" is a necessary compact or compromise between the people from whom power originates, and rulers exercising it. As seen above, the former seek various services that differ according to period and region. The most common:

—reproduction prospects (registry offices regulate the creation and evolution of families);

—internal and external security (police and army);

—an equitable handling of conflicts with authority or other members of the community (courts);

—a distribution of wealth and public responsibilities (taxation and regulation) allowing reasonable subsistence and lodging prospects.

In exchange, individuals surrender much authority to rulers, and *inevitably* lose a corresponding part of their individual and civic freedom.

This last element is major and affects everything else; it rests on the close and adversarial relationship between security and freedom. It's universally recognized that the state's first duty is to ensure the security of its subjects; it's the first need to be satisfied and without it none of the others can be fulfilled. Specifically, from the liberal point of view, genuine freedom is impossible without a certain measure of security; it creates the need for "rule of law" in the first place, to eliminate tyranny and anarchy, and to protect the right to private property, the principal incarnation of freedom.

On the other hand, common sense dictates there couldn't be genuine security without limitations to freedom. The following is a simple demonstration: security can assume two forms, exterior and interior, whose nature is easy to understand if they're respectively represented by a battlement and a handrail. The former protects against others, the latter against oneself; the first restricts the movement and therefore the freedom of those on the outside, the second circumscribes the action of those on the inside. Our societies' laws and institutions include both types, be they combined or separate: the former is represented by the army, laws controlling immigration or punishing criminal behavior; the latter by traffic police, laws against suicide, those concerning drugs and alcohol, etc. Accordingly, there must be a double constraint on freedom that is somewhat pronounced, depending on whether security measures are more severe and therefore more effective.

That ambiguous relation between freedom and security is succinctly described in Wendell Phillip's aphorism "The price of freedom is eternal vigilance," i.e., eternal insecurity; the problem is finding out whether nations are ready to pay that price, or if they can be equitably compelled to do so. In its passion for individual freedom, the discourse concerning American-style democracy (which for the moment gives the tone to the rest of the world) completely ignores the social contract's fundamental nature as a compromise, and the philosophical fact that freedom and security are more contradictory than complementary. The consequences of this omission are much greater than we could imagine. And so, we'd like citizens everywhere to confer the same minimal functions to the state, while preserving all their freedoms. But circumstances (economic necessities and threats to security in particular) and customs aren't the same everywhere; the structural and functional imbalances that result, clearly explain the disorder and even the brutal rejection of democracy we often witness in newer countries.

A PROBLEM OF POWER

The prevalent view of the state during antiquity, even among advocates of democracy like Solon and Pericles, was that it had to be totalitarian, since the need for order and security was far more pressing than the danger of oppression from a power that was still in infancy. Moreover, the Greek definition of freedom is significant: the right to obey the law. "The state had a liberating effect. It freed the citizen from subjugation to individuals, groups or specific claims, while demanding that he transfer to it the sum of his previous devotions," writes Jean Touchard in his "Histoires des idées politiques." Therefore, political power wasn't a danger to freedom; on the contrary, it created and guaranteed it. However, it demanded recognition of its authority in exchange. This idea survived unchanged throughout the history of the West until the mid 18th century (it's found in Montesquieu), even under the oppression of sovereigns; this was considered not as a denial of the rule, but as an offence against "natural law."

John Locke and Jean-Jacques Rousseau were the first to propose the idea of specific protection for the individual against state tyranny. Their initial goal was to combat, not so much misuse of power, but abuse arising from the capriciousness of absolute monarchs; their rationale: in a "state of nature," man is completely free. This illusion was understandable at a time when belief in the "noble savage" still existed. However, ethnology has taught us a great deal since: the "state of nature" is a complete fiction; man, even the most primitive, is found only in groups, where a primitive form of authority already exists; and slavery is one of the oldest known social relations.

The American Thomas Jefferson and the Englishman John Stuart Mill went one step further, saying freedom is a right in itself that must be protected from any violation, including the actions of a government representing a sovereign people (tyranny of the majority). Both associated that idea to the "pursuit of happiness," an expression clearly expressed in the American Declaration of Independence. As well, they believed that pursuit of happiness should be completely unfettered.

Why this sudden shift and insistence on a new and radical definition of freedom, which finally became the dominant theme of Western political evolution, although it's found nowhere else in the world? Because, according to the definition of democracy then formulated, power lay not in the hands of the people, but in those of a much more insular social class. The right to vote in the West was, at first, narrowly linked to ownership of property. It only applied to citizens who could demonstrate a certain level of wealth or ownership of land. The same rule determined who had the right to be elected.

The West's "democratic revolution," which largely occurred between 1780 and 1880, had the primary goal and result of toppling the existing monarchic and aristocratic order and replacing it with the authority of owners, i.e., mainly members of the bourgeoisie. Once established, they had no intention of allowing the popular masses—their necessary ally in the preceding phase—to depose them in turn; they therefore devised mechanisms ensuring their grasp would endure. The first and most important one was representativeness.

In republics of antiquity, authority continued to belong to the citizen, who could at any time take it back from leaders and confer it to others; this was a "delegative" democracy where the independence of individuals was guaranteed by their right to intervene directly in political affairs. On the other hand, citizens in our system can't delegate power temporarily. They surrender it once and for all and then have no purpose in the governmental mechanism, save as taxpayers and occasionally as electors who choose their next leaders. That's what we call "representative" democracy: our elected representatives are the rightful owners of power and exercise it as they see fit. They're only accountable at the end of their mandate.

This notion is intimately linked to the "rule of law" principle already mentioned, with the usual justification that it protects the volatile multitude against its own impulsiveness. The more elitist explanation given by most authors is that the multitude, ignorant and swayed by passion, is incapable of the reasoning needed for making political decisions. In the modern era, we've added that the increasing size of nations would render the idea of "direct" democracy unworkable, even if it were desirable.

This absence of popular control over the state could occasion a new form of despotism, that would tarnish the system's legitimacy and make it more difficult to swallow by the population. That's why the first democratic regimes (United States and France) strove to restore the equilibrium by specifically recognizing the right to armed insurrection, should abuse of power occur. That's the origin of the "right to bear arms," granted to everyone by the American Constitution—a right that's worthless today, given the imbalance between the state's immense arsenal and the more modest firearms owned by individuals; however, it was meaningful when the constitution was framed.

Constitutional drafters eliminated the highly explosive notion of legitimate insurrection from most documents very early on. On the other hand, inspired by Locke and especially Stuart Mill, they provided individual freedom with guarantees that seem to make it an absolute even above the sovereignty of nations. Nowadays, for example, the UN Charter insists that these guarantees be the same everywhere and sets very high standards in principle. As well, that charter leaves the "sovereign will" of peoples no latitude to determine the compromise it feels to be the most desirable between state power and freedom of the citizen.

Things differ in practice: as might be expected, the degree to which liberties are restricted is directly proportional to the prominence of the role given each state and varies considerably from one to the next according to culture and degree of evolution. England, the "cradle of democracy," deviates from the rule: it allows Parliament to control and modify all laws, including the Constitution; and its supreme tribunal has only the status of a parliamentary committee with power to recommend. In formal terms, therefore, individual rights there are more poorly protected than, for example, those in Iran ... while in reality custom offers them better protection than almost anywhere else in the world.

You may think I'm spending too much time on this point; that even if the "state of nature" were fiction, it still provided the individual an unprecedented degree of freedom. Be patient. I only want to demonstrate, in a first instance, that freedom was posited as an "absolute" (as desirable as that may be) in response to a practical need and that it's based on a misapprehension caused by circumstances that are specific to an era and culture; second, I'll underline how its use can be dangerous and contradictory.

Whether individual rights provide the system with an unassailable foundation is therefore a question that deserves special attention. We'll return to it from another angle in the next chapter. Let's just say it's difficult to debate this idea objectively, at a time when numerous defenders of freedom clamor their indignation (sometimes rightly, I admit) loudly and eloquently, leaving little room for the rather boring voice of reason.

WHAT ROLE THE STATE?

Paradoxically, though from opposing perspectives, both leading Western ideologies have seemingly conspired to minimize the role of public authority in a democracy. For Marxists, the liberal state exists to protect the propertied class; the only way to establish long-term freedom is to abolish it. Most capitalists believe the state must only ensure the freedom of citizens and the protection of private property. They feel the less the state does the better, because it provides them a free hand to maximize profits; some even sincerely believe this is to the greatest benefit of the greatest number (that's the recently fashionable "trickle-down" theory).

But if we rely on the preceding, it's more logical and useful, to our understanding at least, to link the nature and extent of the state's influence to the social contract, and therefore to the needs a majority of the governed wants satisfied. Although groups sometimes succeed in leading this majority to adopt their views, thereby distorting the picture, that doesn't prevent this approach from offering a more flexible, realistic and less sectarian view of the question.

We immediately perceive that some functions, notably those pertaining to the structural satisfaction of primary human needs, arise from the very nature of society (they emerge from what was known as "natural law" during the Enlightenment); they are part of the basic social contract and are always defined in constitutions as rightfully belonging to public authorities. They specifically include internal and external security, justice, tax collection, registry offices.

Of course, there are many examples where some of these tasks were delegated to private bodies or even individuals. In monarchic Europe, officials literally bought their appointments, afterwards treating them as personal property they could bequeath to their children; some lucrative but unpopular functions such as tax collecting were farmed out to independent businessmen. Closer to home, certain U.S. states have experimented with contracting out the management of prisons and the power to distribute fines. The Catholic clergy in Quebec has until recently administered most registry offices (births, marriages, deaths), while justice is the exclusive domain of religious leaders in numerous Muslim countries.

There are three distinct replies to these exceptions, as the case may be. The venality of appointments didn't result from popular will, but from the avarice or financial needs of sovereigns; it was unanimously contested and reproved. Farming out and contracting assign work to the exterior, but the primary responsibility remains with the state; anyhow, they've generally proven costly and ineffective when they concern public activities. Finally, wherever the clergy has a direct role in civil administration, no separation of church and state exists; therefore, to all practical purposes the religious hierarchy is treated as a simple extension of the government hierarchy or vice versa.

A second category includes tasks (not clearly considered as basic needs) that are beyond the ability of individuals or families, or require impartial arbitration: roads, public transportation, regulation of health and trade, education. The practice here varies from one nation to the other; however, in most cases these tasks tend to be delegated to public authorities and are often accompanied by parallel private mechanisms.

Other functions, finally, depend on historical, economic or geographical circumstances and the way they're regulated can therefore vary widely from one state to the next. For example, whether a country enjoys self-sufficiency in the production of food visibly determines the level of public intervention in agriculture. State participation and regulatory activity will be more or less pronounced, according to the nature of the main economic activity (extraction of resources, heavy industry, high technology, international trade and finance). Even in very liberal Western countries, a war is all the reason needed for the emergence of state-planned production and for freedom of speech and information, the most fundamental one in our democracy, to be curtailed and shadowed.

Psychological and cultural realities must also be considered. Our view of the social contract isn't strictly limited to immediate material interests; it's clearly affected by our background and way of thinking. Although these are, in turn, obviously influenced by economic realities, that doesn't mean they have no independence or can't survive long outside the conditions that created them. Authors such as Max Weber and R.H. Tawney have convincingly demonstrated Christianity's role—particularly that of English Protestantism—in the evolution of democracy.

Other regions of the world may have widely differing leanings and expectations, simply because of subjective cultural distinctions. It's obvious, for example, that any study of the Indian subcontinent's chaotic evolution which ignores religious, ethnic and caste-structure problems would provide a very incomplete and even distorted picture of nearly one-fifth of mankind, while nonetheless respecting all the rules of economic analysis. Likewise, the carving-up of Black Africa (at the 1885 Berlin Conference) to suit colonial interests, while ignoring tribal realities, has meant the continent is the perennial victim of tremors that undermine its social and economic welfare.

My purpose isn't to take stock of all these differences and imbalances. I must, however, distinctly underscore that the current argument favoring a minimalist view of the state, and its non-intervention in the economic order, only has a solid material and cultural base in a limited number of countries and for a relatively brief duration. Far from resolving problems, its application in the rest of the world, and in the long-term, runs the serious risk of exacerbating them and especially of provoking an explosive divorce between the views of peoples still immersed in specific practical and sociological realities, and those of their governments, alienated by a europeanized and technical education. Before moving on to another theme, it's important to glance at the principal mechanism used to defend and practically impose this minimalist and globalist reasoning, that of international bodies and, in the highest degree, the United Nations.

THE "NEW OLIGARCHICAL ORDER"

While free-world powers pay lip service to the need for respecting liberal democratic rules in every state, they're erecting a "new world order" based on completely different mechanisms. The UN Charter clearly enunciates principles concerning the sovereignty of peoples and the right to free elections by secret ballot. In practice, when it doesn't invoke these principles to justify somewhat shady operations, it frequently ignores them and does the opposite of what it preaches, by resorting to practices having definite oligarchical tendencies.

First, the admission and maintenance of a state in the UN practically ignore adherence to those ideals, focusing instead on recognizing "legitimacy" which in fact boils down to ownership of power. Were all the countries that broke its most basic rule, following a coup d'État or other misadventure, to be suspended from the organization, few seats in the Assembly hall would be occupied. Statistically, countries with popularly elected governments remain a clear minority.

Second, by imposing rigid guarantees concerning citizens' rights (inspired by Western reasoning and ignoring the development level of each political society), the UN clearly contradicts its own principle advocating the respect of national sovereignties and the sacred right to national self-determination. Even assuming those guarantees are universally valid, a strategy based on factors such as accepting each nation's evolution, the repercussions of popular education, and the example provided by more advanced countries, might provide less-immediate results, but they'd be more durable than those obtained by the violent methods now used.

Third, the only really "democratic" arm of United Nations, the General Assembly, has no executory power; its role is strictly consultative. The Security Council is the decision-making branch. Its permanent membership includes three Western democracies, the U.S., France and the U.K.—an oligarchical club—which, by a happy coincidence provide most of the organization's funding. The other permanent members are China and Russia. Temporary members are in principle chosen through a sort of co-optation by their permanent counterparts; without the agreement of the latter, no country stands a chance of being admitted. A good example: although Japan and Germany have all the qualifications needed, their efforts to open up the club have so far been futile; the most ironic is that once they get in, they'll be hand in glove for maintaining the "status quo." It's no wonder most Latin-American countries vigorously demanded reform in the midsummer of 1993, arguing that two continents are over-represented where it counts at the UN—Europe (three permanent members) and North America (one out of three countries)—while all others are practically absent.

Finally, ballot secrecy isn't observed by any branch of the international organization; it's more important to know the identity of "friends and enemies," than to allow the more vulnerable countries to act according to their conscience or interest, without fear of reprisals.

Another current example of the new world order's oligarchical tendency, on the economic level, is found in the GATT, the General Agreement on Tariffs and Trade. Its evolution since the 1950s has revealed a tendency of imposing a commercial trading model based on a Western and industrial concept that will likely maintain or even increase the gap between rich and poor. For example, the rules it is ready to implement will bluntly prevent young countries from adopting growth strategies (self-capitalization, temporary protection of internal markets, coordinated state planning) that were so beneficial to Japan and the "four tigers" of East Asia, and the only ones to have proven their durability and efficiency for underdeveloped countries over the last decades.

Many Third-World economists and administrators emphasize that "globalization of trade" is almost exclusively advocated by members of the Group of Seven and that the rest of mankind can only submit to it. They recognize two rarely mentioned defects:

a) the disappearance of barriers and regulations on the import-export of food will deny states control of their agriculture. Moreover, the obligation of providing food for the population is, with ensuring its security, the very first duty and the very first measure of a country's sovereignty. It isn't surprising that most promoters of this aspect of the GATT are self-sufficient and even produce excess, and that its detractors experience shortages. It would be interesting to see, for example, whether the United States would remain such a fervent advocate of government non-intervention in agriculture, if it ever became dependent on food imports.

b) Wherever industrial infrastructures are weak or nonexistent, implementation of the GATT has already ensured that the only local businesses to prosper are those that import, while most manufacturing of goods (which is nearly always modest) is achieved by capital originating and controlled from the exterior. In both cases, the net result is not enrichment, but an impoverishment of the country's economy by a flight of currency, either through foreign purchases or profit taking. "Compensation" in the form of salaries paid to the country's workers is most often far from adequate. Although not an economist, I've personally observed the dramatic extent of that phenomenon, notably in Algeria and in some Black-African countries.

Even by limiting myself to this rapid overview, I believe I've demonstrated the extent to which the "new world order," extolled by the club of so-called democratic nations, pays little attention to the sovereignty of peoples or to some of the fundamental values it ascribes to democracy.

MORAL OR PRACTICAL JUSTIFICATION

The democratic concept has been defended from a moral perspective for over a century: some have alleged it was the only way to ensure respect for the social contract between people and leaders, and to protect individual freedoms against the abuse of power. But the more we study the mechanism and its effects, the more we realize that neither morality nor justice have much to do with it. It's acknowledged that everywhere, with the possible exception of Germany (which in any event wasn't a democracy at the time, but an "enlightened" despotic regime), pressure from unions and the people, and fear of socialism—not liberal principles—have led to most measures pertaining to economic equity and social security. Moreover, governments have found numerous methods to skirt the "freedom of the individual" rule or turn it against itself, to expand and reinforce their authority wherever they felt the need.

That's why the "moral" dimension is now absent from the arguments of the system's most lucid defenders: they don't advocate it because it's good or just, but solely because they believe democracy works. Their case quickly boils down to arguing that Western peoples have never been so powerful and prosperous. Mistaking the effect (democracy) for the cause (prosperity) doesn't seem to bother them. Their position was rather easy to defend from the end of the Second World War to the oil crises of the 1970s and 80s; it's somewhat less so today and they no longer tend to fall back on a comparison with the past but, instead, with societies that haven't known the same state of grace.

Unfortunately, the proof is here again less and less certain. A study conducted by Harvard economists into the conditions needed for a country to escape underdevelopment clearly demonstrates a preference for an authoritarian political regime, rather than an exemplary democracy. Recent success stories in this area—Taiwan, South Korea, Hungary, Pinochet's Chili and especially Red China—bear this out. It's even symptomatic for some of these countries, once they've achieved prosperity, to suddenly discover democratic inclinations, as was recently highlighted in an article by sinologist Jules Nadeau. He and others conclude in favor of a universal adoption of democracy; in my opinion, this only provides further proof that, unfortunately, democracy is a luxury for (newly) rich countries, rather than a prescription for the success of poorer ones.

The purpose of this chapter was to examine the relationship between political structure and fundamental social needs, as represented by the "social contract." Democracy is clearly one of the solutions we've devised, the least inadequate until now, to legitimize those links; however, nothing proves it's the only one. We've also seen how ideas that were originally foreign to democracy (representativeness, individual rights and freedoms) grafted themselves to it, forming an inseparable whole, because of conditions peculiar to a time and region of the world. The problem is that those ideas eventually contradict the premises of democratic ideology and yield consequences that imperil the system's efficiency and ultimately its existence.

-3-

A SOCIETY AT WAR
WITH ITSELF

In a world where our lives unfold at the rhythm of information bulletins and headlines, the daily news reveals a painful and variegated procession of social conflicts: peaceful or violent demonstrations, Turkish or Bosnian immigrants, gays and lesbians, cod fishermen; condemnation of government actions by environmentalists, complaints of a minority before the courts. From one year to the next, we observe that these quarrels increase, intensify and become inflamed. Some argue this is an illusion created by the media. They're deluding themselves, making the timeless mistake of confusing message and messenger. We live in a society that's increasingly adversarial; this is directly linked to the democratic system.

A chronic social problem is the inevitable and regular confrontation between the citizen's desires and the necessities of collective interest. Obviously, the state can't satisfy everybody at once, except in cases of great abundance and an extremely homogenous population. It must then either abdicate its role, or make difficult choices to ensure its survival and vigor, which it rightly or wrongly associates to that of the nation. By so doing, it eventually hinders the interests of groups or individuals that make up society. I believe Lester Thurow is the author who's best described that dilemma in "The Zero-Sum Society." But, he doesn't fully perceive the extent of what he uncovers, likely because he's an economist: he examines the financial and sometimes legal aspects, but ignores social and political implications.

Although the problem isn't new, it's critical to liberal regimes. Based on the opposing views of Jean-Jacques Rousseau and John Locke, the nature and extent of individual freedom, as opposed to the imperatives of popular will, played a prominent role in the debates of the French and American revolutions at the end of the 18th century. The solutions adopted on both sides of the Atlantic were very different and had almost completely opposite results. The French placed sovereignty in the nation and subordinated the interests of citizens to it. The Americans bestowed authority on the people, who legitimize the government, and limited the state's role to that of guardian of individual rights and happiness. Traces of Rousseau's theory, concerning the primacy of "collective will" and the importance of the nation, are still found in France and other Latin countries; but nowadays, the Anglo-American individualist approach prevails, particularly from the United Nations' supranational perspective.

What's the relationship between this situation and the political system? To understand it, many aspects of the question must be examined; though distinct, they are significantly integrated and difficult to treat separately: the primacy of individual rights, minimal and "manager-style" government, the absence of a consensus about public interest, the proliferation of pressure groups, and the adjudication of disputes by the courts.

THE INDIVIDUAL ABOVE ALL

We've seen how and why "individual rights" permeated democratic principles and mechanisms in general. On the one hand, this provided ordinary citizens with solid guarantees against the tyranny of a state dominated by a political oligarchy. On the other, it offered a practical response to the persistent problem concerning the moral legitimacy and the application of rules devised by popularly elected assemblies.

Its present incarnation was inspired by John Stuart Mill, who posited individual freedom as the supreme imperative, even above the satisfaction of hunger—which, according to his reasoning, must be achieved through capitalism's beneficial effects, not the state. The most straightforward formulation of this idea is found in a U.S. Supreme Court ruling (Oliver Wendell Holmes) from the mid-nineteenth century: freedoms can only be limited when they "place the state in clear and present danger."

That view is reflected in the charters of rights that serve as preambles to various constitutions. In most countries, and for a long time, it hasn't caused serious problems; it only provided a philosophical guideline to legislators, who referred to it more or less to direct their reasoning when they drafted laws. But it has assumed a completely different proportion and significance over the last few decades in the United States, and much more recently elsewhere, with the emergence of pressure groups that use individual rights as a weapon to advance their cause, often contradicting the perception of governments concerning public interest. The creation of constitutional tribunals and an increase in supreme court powers have given greater prominence to that movement.

A typical example is the abortion-rights battle in the United States. Obviously a "societal problem" with important social and economic repercussions, it also raises moral and religious questions. Both sides of this wide-ranging war systematically refer to the individual rights contained in the Constitution and Bill of Rights, thereby practically ignoring the collective and communal aspects. One side pleads the "right to life," while the other argues for "freedom of choice." And the state's role in all this? It carefully remains on the sidelines, declining to even mediate; it specifically refuses to take an active position or to bring political and social considerations into the debate, although it's their designated guardian.

THE MINIMALIST STATE

This attitude is dictated by electoral preoccupations: no party wants to openly alienate important voting blocs represented by each faction. It's also an example of the "minimalist" view of government, which maintains the state is a necessary evil whose intrusion into the lives of citizens must be strictly limited. This theme has often been reiterated in the dominant politico-economic discourses of the last fifteen years. It derives from the "laissez faire, laissez aller" ideas of French physiocrats and British traditionalists like Edmund Burke, and completely satisfies modern conservatives of the Reagan-Thatcher type. In the end, it appears as an immutable truth because it's constantly repeated and linked to a belief popular among taxpayers; namely, that "we pay too many taxes because the government meddles with everything."

Faithful to that narrow view of their purpose, our governments tend to consider themselves strictly as teams of managers who "solve" the individual-community conflict by ignoring it. For the moment, the phenomenon is less obvious in Europe than America, but is clearly making headway in England, Germany and even France (in the tone and in some of the arguments of the debate concerning the fate of illegal immigrants). Instead of making necessary decisions in the name of a public interest they can no longer clearly identify, our leaders finally limit themselves to being passive spectators or, at best, reluctant arbitrators between various private organizations or pressure groups that have their own definition of the public good. Nobody seems to perceive the illogic of this behavior.

The simplest reflection reveals that without an organized community and a politically structured society, there are no possible grounds for "human rights," no individual freedoms save those of the jungle, i.e., survival of the fittest. Liberal theory implicitly admits this by presupposing the rule of law, but denies its unavoidable corollary: government, which is the instrument for the political administration of society, has a positive role to play in the lives of its citizens. That role provides it with rights and obligations to intervene, beyond the purely passive or negative ones presently conceded to it. Not only is the state not a necessary evil, but it's still the only structure that can guarantee and harmonize the rights we have. As such, it must notably promulgate and enforce the rules governing relations between the diverse communities of interest that form a complex society; for the moment, it does this reluctantly and most often by devising those rules through a straightforward extension of individual rights. Worse yet, it tends to leave their creation to courts made up of non-elected specialists, fearing to venture into the political arena and face the anger of activists of every shade and hue.

Enacting laws is the most important of all powers, according to classical democratic theory since Locke and Montesquieu. In modern practice, the state's weakest branch is often the legislature. Save in exceptional cases (like France after the left's collapse in March 1993), parliaments and national assemblies now only rubber stamp executive decisions. And they've largely abdicated their role in setting social norms, leaving this to the courts, which "interpret" existing laws, their own jurisprudence and, as a last resort, charters of rights.

Elected assemblies have increasingly become irrelevant for two reasons: first, the influence of political parties, whose discipline condemns independent thinking by any representatives who aren't a direct part of the executive; second, supreme courts have been given power to uphold or invalidate most parliamentary decisions. There's also a tendency among British-type regimes of enacting "special" short-term laws concerning just about anything, mostly to solve administrative problems; as a result, the law gradually loses its prestige, continuity and legitimacy.

Significantly, in many countries the debate concerning the need to reassert the value of representatives is revived every five or ten years. Some countries have even made efforts in that regard with somewhat mixed results, for a very simple reason: it isn't the representative's role that must be reassessed, it's that of the legislature. That error is another example of our tendency to look at problems from the individual's perspective, while they concern collectivities, groups or institutions. Unless the decision-making power and ability to hold real debates on leading social problems are restored to parliaments, most elected representatives will continue to be little more than ornamental figureheads and handmaids to the executive.

THE PUBLIC INTEREST, THAT UNKNOWN

It seems the only government capable of providing acceptable results in the long-term, even at the level of individual satisfaction, is the one focusing on public interest. On what other basis can it impose the unavoidable compromise between options that are at once desirable and contradictory; for example, environmental protection and economic development as sources of well-being? However, two major obstacles confront leaders wanting to take that path; one practical, the other more philosophical. But both are directly related to basic principles of our democratic system.

The first: a politician who wants to be elected in our system must flatter egoism by campaigning to increase the rights of everyone, without ever mentioning the weakening of collective authority which, as we've seen, is its necessary counterpart. The situation has worsened with the emergence, over the last two decades, of multiple pressure groups and combative minorities. Although their causes are often valid when considered individually, their overall effect is to compel leaders to make decision based on the relative weight of forces at hand, instead of general interest.

The second, and more serious one, is that we've lost sight of what public interest might be, and that to retrieve it our leaders must adopt a much more active and volontarist attitude than the one allowed by the dominant ideology. As our societies become more heterogeneous and open, static consensuses about values often derived from a same religion, ancient customs and a similar education, fragment and disappear. Recognizing this doesn't mean deploring it; this new diversity enriches all of society. But we must also admit that it forces us to recreate, on an infinitely more complex and dynamic basis, a concept of public interest that can be shared by all, and values strong enough to serve as criteria for decisions that are sometimes difficult.

For many, this theme belongs to the "right," since work, religious morality, respect for the family, patriotism, etc., are the subjects most mentioned in an enumeration of those values. But we might just as well evoke community spirit, civic pride, a sense of sharing and solidarity, attitudes usually attributed to the "left," which were very common among most of our parents and grandparents. The main thing is to rediscover or recreate a consensus about public interest that heeds the new diversity of our societies. In any event, we can't dream of recreating an enduring "public interest code," like the one that existed previously; societal changes occur so rapidly and are so varied that they require constant modifications. The best we can hope for is the devising of "transformation rules" able to provide guidelines through this evolution.

The absence of an agreement on this point has two immediate results, whose danger we may not have sufficiently weighed. First, in the void thereby created, the liberal argument that public interest can only arise from the confrontation of individual interests has, by default, assumed the strength of dogma. Well-being and the future are perceived as commodities to be bartered in a sort of free market of ideas. At first glance, this doesn't seem such a bad thing. But we very quickly realize, given the total absence of guidelines, that what matters in this context isn't logic, likelihood, nor even the opinion of a majority of citizens, but the organizational skills, strength of personality, and resources available to those defending a particular position. Second, this approach has created a climate of perpetual confrontation between hostile factions in the community, where the simple citizen, that "individual" whose rights we defend so fiercely, no longer has a voice. He ultimately feels both powerless and stressed by this pitched battle, whose fronts vary from one week or month to the next, but whose intensity is maintained without respite or truce.

A MOSAIC OF MINORITIES

A majority of industrial states, including the most stable, have lost their old uniformity. This is, among other things, due to the intermixing of populations caused by wars, the influx of refugees and economic immigration. Not only do cultures and ethnic groups rub shoulders and intermix on the same territory, but their members increasingly express a desire to assert their own identity: language, rituals, customs, lifestyle. Similarly, various groups often bullied or neglected by the population emerge proclaiming their rights, either to equality, difference, or treatment they believe is more equitable: feminists, homosexuals, the disabled, the elderly, residents of underprivileged neighborhoods ... Add to that alliances created to defend certain causes: ecologists, supporters or opponents of abortion, cyclists, ancient-architecture enthusiasts, public-daycare clients, etc.

This mosaic of minorities may appear as a reaction to the immensity of our societies. Numerous groups and movements arise wishing to carve their place in the community to counterbalance the massive weight of large businesses and gigantic public institutions, against which their members feel powerless; their smaller size and simpler (not to say at times simplistic) views make them communities with which it is easier for the individual to identify. This emotion and tendency can only irritate liberal humanists: they feel compelled to sympathize with any show of protest against the impersonal immensity of the state and multinationals, but the proliferation of minorities grouped on the basis of ethnic, cultural or geographic characteristics goes against the egalitarian and internationalist underpinnings of their philosophy.

Some of these pressure groups exist only briefly, with time enough to achieve their goal or realize it's unreachable; they most often carve themselves a lasting niche in society and become institutions. Sometimes they even acquire prominence and political weight: the Greens in Europe and pro-lifers in the United States. The snag: to assert their demands, which are collective in nature, they mainly rely on rights defined individually in charters and constitutions. In the absence of notions and traditions concerning minority or collective rights, they have little choice and the courts in most countries prove them right. But this is a virtual highjacking of the bill of rights and often a negation of popular sovereignty, which should be the fundamental principle of democracy. Indeed, protection for the citizen's freedom was conceived to prevent the state apparatus from oppressing the individual, and not to serve as a basis for the creation of a "modus vivendi" between a multitude of communities whose interests often conflict. The first inconsistency: those groups often claim that the minority they allegedly incarnate has been the victim of some injustice. They demand rectification or compensation in the name of the rights of those individuals... while it's only possible to prove discrimination on a collective basis. For instance, it's impossible to demonstrate that a particular woman with AIDS is a victim of ostracism; the bad treatment she endures might be attributable to numerous other causes: language, religion, ethnic origin, economic condition or level of education, etc. To establish proof, it's essential to demonstrate that all or an abnormally high number of women with AIDS are submitted to the same treatment. This should normally imply that the remedy needed is also collective, but it so happens our system doesn't recognize that type of solution! This is one of the interesting conclusions Thurow makes in the book mentioned above, but we don't have to accept it as authoritative: the least reflection based on facts will confirm it.

Second, the question of majorities concerns communities, not individuals. Whether a neighborhood contains one Sikh or a half dozen, everyone stares at them with a curiosity often mixed with sympathy. However, if they arrive by the hundreds and insist on wearing turbans, beards, daggers in their belts, and post signs in their language on walls, the pleasant surprise quickly gives way to indignation and public protest— reactions immediately condemned for their racism and religious discrimination. The phenomenon is well known by social workers. The solution is obviously not to confine minorities to ghettos, nor to force them to strictly adapt to the majority's customs. Nor is it to condemn the majority's reaction which, though primal and aggressive, is perfectly natural and involuntary. On the other hand, it's clear we aren't even addressing the problem's essence by trying to resolve it on the basis of freedom of religion, expression, or lifestyle: the conflict is on another level. Despite the claims of classical liberals, of the Pierre Elliott Trudeau ilk, there must be such a thing as "collective rights," with political and legal effects that, far from threatening freedoms, are crucial to their preservation and conciliation.

Third, it would be neither "liberal" nor democratic to give narrow groups, whose representativeness is far from proven, the right to define public interest. Their definitions usually pertain to a rather limited aspect of society: abortion or "right to life," aggressive patriotism or antinuclear belief, help for refugees, condemnation of torture and repression, protection of wild animals, help for victims of a particular catastrophe or illness. There's no question of judging the validity of these "causes," but only of underlining that none of their partisans takes the least pain to evaluate the eventual success of their cause, or compare its merits with those of another group: each is convinced their grievances and legitimacy supersede all others. Since the state refuses to propose a general vision of public interest, which would denote the relative importance of these causes in a global scheme, that perspective has no chance of existing.

But nearly all minorities share three traits, regardless of their ideology or the justness of their cause. First, they pretend to speak for the entire community, if not for all mankind, while they represent only a fraction. Second, their attitude is often earmarked by intolerance and their actions nearly always involve confrontation, either with groups whose ideas they oppose, or with public authorities who are both the villain and the source of money and power they need to achieve their ends. Third, they have very quickly learned to use the judicial system, either to be proven right, or to delay or prevent any decision not in their favor, even by paralyzing processes that are perceived as essential to public interest by the majority.

OMNIPOTENT SERVANTS

This brings us to the last part of the question: more of our problems and disagreements are now settled before the courts... and more time is needed to handle them. The frequently and acutely deplored slowness of our legal system is primarily caused by increasingly elaborate procedures, as well as laws and jurisprudence that are more numerous and open to varying, if not contradictory, interpretations. This is partly attributable to the increasing complexity of our societies, the abdication of legislative power, and to the considerable (not to say exaggerated) importance we now confer to the notion of rights.

Those three causes were assessed separately above. We must now describe the relations between them to better understand the vicious circle that results from their interaction. This tends to exacerbate each of their characteristics, leading to a kind of dictatorship of the judiciary on all our lives, a result far removed from the original objectives of liberal thinkers.

Obviously, the "right to be different," based on freedom of thought, expression and action, can only lead to a heterogeneous and complex society, except where extremely strong social pressure in favor of conformity cancels their effect, as was once the case in some of the most conservative regions of the United States and Europe. However, there is, even in those areas, a clear and perceptible tendency towards the differentiation of certain minorities on a linguistic, ethnic, sexual or ideological basis. In the past, isolated individuals didn't dare brave the strength of a monolithic (often narrow-minded) public opinion. Today, organized groups, relying on explicit provisions of constitutions or the general protection offered by charters, do so with increasing success.

These groups shatter the traditional and simplistic consensus about public interest; in turn, politicians seeking re-election must consider the voting blocs they represent. Confronted by this new double reality, elected assemblies, already denied most of their authority by the concentration of power in the executive, have a natural tendency of not legislating and leaving responsibility to arbitrate unavoidable conflicts to the courts.

The legal system, however, doesn't work by considering logic or common sense, nor by making decisions according to public interest. It would obviously be unfair to claim it's opposed to those concepts; it simply operates according to other principles, codified as procedural rules, whose commendable goal is to reduce human arbitrariness in the exercise of justice to an absolute minimum. Those principles consist of a strict interpretation of existing rights, a respect for jurisprudence and rules concerning proof. In other words, resorting to the courts reduces most decisions to a literal and quasi-mechanical use of individual rights ... which completes the vicious circle.

Therefore, not only do we increasingly find ourselves before the courts, but more and more people adopt the same legalistic attitude, to prevent the risk of having to justify their actions to them. This is not only the case for bureaucrats and public representatives, but for numerous large-business executives, members of liberal professions, merchants ... So much so, that many disputes previously resolved through mutual agreement and common sense, now find themselves in a quasi-judicial context as soon as they appear: car collisions, brawls between drunks, family disputes, etc.

This has three injurious effects. First, it transforms magistrates, who ought to serve justice and the public, into all-powerful masters of society's operating principles, although they're often uneasy in that role. Second, it exacerbates social tensions by greatly complicating daily life through a multiplication of rules, duties and prohibitions, for which the government is exclusively and wrongfully held responsible: the red tape scorned by our American friends. Ironically, they don't realize that red tape is a nearly unavoidable result of their passion for individual rights and that any efforts to reduce the size and influence of government runs the risk of increasing it further. Third, it further impedes the course of justice, already congested with minor cases its apparatus was never designed to settle individually.

AN ADVERSARIAL SOCIETY

The foregoing contains repetitions and redundancies for a very simple reason: although each of the realities described has a specific existence, there are major connections between them that make it impossible to describe one without mentioning the others in the same breath. However, it was necessary to display them separately to better expose the workings of the mechanism that leads to communal conflict.

A sixth piece of the puzzle is missing: the economic value imposed on all things, even the most intangible. Examples abound: the monetary value ascribed to pollution, to a physician's professional error, to a rape, or the abuse of child by his parents. When will murder be compensated by the "cost of a human life?" Some companies have already done this (Union Carbide for the Bhopal tragedy in India). It's obvious and significant that our society is returning to the old tribal practice, long considered barbaric and inhuman, of exacting the "price of blood" through economic liberalism. This notion is clearly part of our equation; however, it's more relevant to a critique of capitalism than democracy, and that's why I only mention it briefly.

Does this mean that other fundamental elements of an adversarial society are consequences of democracy? In varying ways and degrees, without a doubt. Two of its most explicit and revered pillars are the primacy of individual rights and their foundation, the rule of law. The minimalist view of government and the legislature's passivity are direct results of electioneering and the pre-eminence of the individual over the community. The growth in size and strength of active minorities is caused by the unavoidable giantism of institutions to which intellectual liberalism leads—an effect to be studied in a subsequent chapter; it's favored by a broad interpretation of individual rights and the passive attitude of elected representatives concerning public interest. Finally, a greater reliance on the courts arises from the existence of those minorities and the enshrining of individual rights.

It remains to be determined to what extent those effects are unavoidable, or whether it's possible to mitigate or even eliminate them without challenging the entire democratic system. I haven't tried to establish irrefutable logical proof of this aspect; but, in my opinion, all the clues we have point in the same direction: there's a causal relation that can't be modified without changing the basic terms. For instance, while the need to elevate the role of elected representatives, and mitigate the intervention of the judiciary in daily life, has been emphasized for decades, the opposite continues to happen, as if these phenomena were unavoidable effects of the system. The more we curtail the state's role, and find other avenues for groups and minorities to express themselves, the less conflicts are settled, and the more they become complicated and inflamed. It's normal and healthy for those conflicts to exist; they're the result of a pluralist society and open the way to progress and dynamism. The problem is the system doesn't provide us with the tools needed to solve them, or at least to help them evolve in a direction beneficial to the entire community.

In antiquity, the notion of democracy held that citizenship was a privilege whose benefits were largely implied, but whose civic duties were clearly defined; in fact, the citizen belonged more to the state than the state to the citizen. That perspective could only appear "totalitarian" to moderns; it effectively thwarted the French interpretation of freedom as expressed by Jean-Jacques Rousseau. Although the liberal-inspired Anglo-American scheme inverted those parameters (our view of citizenship is all rights, few obligations), passage from one extreme to the other entailed inevitable errors of perspective. Between the legalistic interpretation of the Charter and endless pressure-group battles, the notion of public interest, which is essential to the concept of government (whatever form it takes) has practically disappeared from the picture. Restoring it to a system that routinely favors primacy of the individual over the community, is perhaps the unsolvable problem of modern states.

_4_

WHY VOTE?

A pillar of the democratic system is the axiom "one citizen, one vote." It's generally ascribed the following meaning: each citizen has a right to vote solely because he's a citizen, without discrimination based on sex, economic condition, ethnic origin, religious belief, etc.; second, each citizen's vote is equal to that of any other. Philosophically, this rests on the principle of equality between men, which is peculiar to the Christian West and based on the idea that all are "equal before God," and on the typically Protestant notion of free will, which implies the right and responsibility for individuals to make their own choices. In practical terms, we gradually reached this condition after realizing other systems either led to flagrant injustice for certain segments of the population, or to insurmountable implementation problems.

However, that rule has always been flouted by those who were first to promote it; so-called democratic societies have concluded that, taken literally, it produced results that were unacceptable and even absurd. During the 19th century, it was believed that granting voting rights to all meant placing the country's fate in the hands of a majority of ignorant workers, whom it was feared would "yield to their selfish inclinations and to a summary notion of their own interests, against justice and at the expense of all other classes as well as prosperity"; paradoxically, that description is from John Stuart Mill, one of the first great promoters of universal suffrage. Nowadays, there's a thriving "school of apathy" which maintains, for similar reasons, that the less the public is involved in politics, the better off the democratic system will be.

As a result, various means are used to dissuade citizens from voting, or to ensure the voice of each is not equal in practice. And if we count countries where people are directly or indirectly prevented from voting for reasons of sex, age, race, religion or social status, we realize they constitute an immense majority. We may therefore rightly ask if these multiple deviations are unfortunate accidents or if they aren't rather inherent characteristics of democracy and a manifestation of its internal contradictions.

THE FICTION OF UNIVERSALITY

I've already mentioned that the inventors of democracy opposed suffrage for women and usually insisted that citizenship be based on property: only adult males that had assets and paid taxes could vote. Depending on the country, between three and eight generations were needed to achieve universal suffrage. For example, American blacks obtained the right to vote throughout the country in 1870, but this was only realized in practice in the middle of the 1960s, with the disappearance of "literacy tests" in the southern states. As for women, they obtained it in 1920, about 140 years after the creation of the republic. During the early nineteenth century in England, James Mill had very seriously proposed the vote be given only to men aged forty and older; anyhow, in those days barely one-sixth of adult English males voted. Finally, in Switzerland, Europe's oldest republic, women first took part in a political decision in 1959—although not in all parts of the country.

The evolution towards universality is generally depicted as an irreversible and continuous movement towards greater openness and equality. In reality, successive concessions were usually acquired through intense struggles. Ruling oligarchies would only make changes once they were sure the "lowly people" wouldn't use those new rights to topple the elite in power or redistribute wealth to its advantage. It therefore seems unjust to say the least, and probably unrealistic, to compel countries that haven't experienced the same evolution to adopt straight out a formula which, in our case, established itself slowly and with multiple hesitations, even among the most enlightened souls.

Today, we seldom mention that between a third and half of the population can't participate in the electoral process: although they're equal and full citizens in principle, children don't have voting rights, even by proxy. The age at which an individual was felt to have passed from childhood to adulthood has varied considerably from one era to another, from one region to the next; for instance, with television and the pervasiveness of the media, many eight year olds are today better informed about the world and their country's government than were most adults, even educated ones, a generation or two ago. Moreover, the age factor is assessed differently according to whether the vote, marriage (or sexual consent) or the payment of taxes are considered. Americans are notorious in this regard for flagrantly violating the sacred principle of "No taxation without representation," although it had given birth to their democratic revolution two centuries ago: celebrity child actors and singers are taxed but can't vote.

Why do we assume the right to vote must be universal? There are two distinct schools of thought on this question: either that right is an intrinsic part of the numerous privileges granted citizens, regardless of their aptitude to exercise it, or it's only given to adults considered able to make rational decisions about political situations.

In the first case, it's abnormal for minors, the insane and common-law prisoners (depending on the country) to be deprived of it, as though they had forfeited their civil rights, or as though there were many unequal categories of citizens. In the second case, it would be natural for us to have the means of validating the competence of electors as is done, for example, before granting citizenship to an immigrant. However, the rules in most countries respect neither of these ideas, but straddle both. On the one hand, it's considered absurd to allow children to vote (while giving the right to senile seniors) even by proxy; on the other, competence tests have been used too often as a pretext to forbid underprivileged or despised groups of citizens to vote, so much so that the practice has been almost completely abandoned.

THE FICTION OF EQUALITY

Even in states where a fairly comprehensive view of equality is accepted, there remains a temptation to deny different categories of citizens their full share of influence in an election, either to help a party or tendency cling to power, or to confer additional importance to social classes considered more responsible or stable. The principal techniques used to circumvent the equality of votes are the distribution of ridings, the single-ballot majority mechanism, and encouraging apathy, notably through an increase in registration formalities and voting procedures.

Wherever voting occurs in ridings, cantons, districts or other territorial zones, boundaries have been changed to modify the relative importance of certain segments of the electorate. For instance, instead of demarcating compact and geographically or socially "natural" territories, electoral boundaries have a tendency of adopting illogical or whimsical layouts, whose true purpose is to include or exclude pockets of electors favorable or inimical to candidates in power. This method is especially visible on electoral maps of semi-urban areas in the middle of the United States, where the size and shape of districts seem to defy all logic, since the territory itself is flat and state boundaries are ruler straight. At the same time, the more traditional ridings and cantons, as well as wealthy neighborhoods, are frequently given a limited size, whereas sectors populated by the urban proletariat, which is potentially more volatile and revolutionary, have far more numerous electoral lists. Since each district elects only one representative, these methods maximize the probability of having a majority of "right-thinking" members; but in so doing, each rural or bourgeois vote is given the value of two or three proletarian ballots. An extreme example of this technique was probably England's "ghost ridings," where a smattering of electors who didn't even live in those districts, could counter the effect of tens of thousands of votes from the populous districts of Birmingham or London's East End.

Voting method results must be added to these territorial aberrations. Electoral-technique specialists have observed that direct voting without proportionality ("winner take all") allows only the votes of those who supported the winner to count, while others have no effect. For example, if a candidate wins with the support of 51% of votes where two-thirds of citizens cast their ballots—which is not unusual—a representative or senator will have been elected by barely a third of electors; the voting rights of the other two-thirds will in no way be represented in the assembly's composition or in the choice of leaders. The increasing tendency throughout the world is to follow that model in the name of government stability. Even France has abandoned the proportional method and returned to a two ballot majority vote. We'll see further on how the voting method is linked to various factors, particularly the number of parties in contention; for now, suffice it to say it influences the relative value of citizens' votes.

Finally, it's altogether ironic that voting is mandatory especially where it has the least significance, in single-party and single-list regimes, and that it's more optional, not to say discouraged, wherever it can have the most effect, in the United States for example. Until recently, in most socialist countries, draconian rules resulted in participation rates that often exceeded 95% simply to confirm a decision having no possible alternative; in the U.S.A., where representatives and senators aren't submitted to party discipline and play a very active role, and where the president, elected by universal suffrage, has quasi-dictatorial powers, it's extremely rare that 50% of citizens vote ... and some political scientists applaud this, arguing the less the public is involved, the better democracy functions.

MATURITY OR DYNAMISM

It's obvious that the universality and equality of votes, already more or less respected in Western Countries of European lineage, are among the democratic principles that pose the most problems when attempts are made to introduce a representative electoral system in other cultures. This is especially true in parts of the world that haven't inherited worship of the individual from Christianity, or Protestantism more specifically. Factors that have an obvious influence on the acceptance or refusal of these notions include: respect for social or political authority, family structures, the existence of castes, and the separation or confusion of the religious and secular.

Universality causes problems at various levels, but first clashes with the "domestic" role assigned to women in numerous cultures—something that hasn't entirely disappeared from ours. The political arena is usually reserved to men, even in regions where little is made of sexual differences on a daily basis. Correcting this situation legally, without changing its underlying mentality, will at best create a class of "captive" women electors who would literally follow the instructions of their fathers or husbands, effectively granting them an extra vote. At worst, this threatens to destroy existing social structures and create a disorder contrary to the desired result, and often detrimental to improving the status of women.

The equality of individual votes seems especially absurd where custom bestows respect on elders for the wisdom they've acquired through experience. This is the case for numerous societies, where some kind of elders' council is part of the ancestral political culture; it's especially true in countries that, contrary to Europe, were acquainted very early on with a primitive form of democracy or a monarchy tempered by the weight of public opinion. For example, this formula was common among North American natives and coexisted

69

with the hereditary or elected tribal and village chief system in Black Africa, before the arrival of Europeans.

This "senatorial" approach is admittedly more suited to static communities that evolve very slowly; it responds with difficulty to the need for rapid change characterizing modern states. It may lead to conservatism and immobilism, since seniors have a natural proclivity to caution and a respect for tradition. For instance, a senate formula is often used to temper and curb the ardor of elected lower houses in the more dynamic Western societies.

The classical Western argument against the approach directly favoring experience, holds that influence must be given to youths by granting them equality of votes, while allowing the moral authority of elders to be wielded through public opinion. This encourages a moderate influx of new and daring ideas into the system, which are a natural source of progress. In practice, the generally conservative class holding power uses all means possible to diminish the effects of this factor. For example, there's a chronic tendency in numerous countries to "forget" student voters when electoral lists are drawn up, or to impose residency requirements that prevent many from voting. And wherever elections occur on a work-day, young employees often discover they have more difficulty than their elders obtaining leave to exercise their democratic right.

The equality of votes may be useful, even necessary, in a society undergoing rapid progress, since it ascribes greater importance to innovation than to the more static dimension of experience. However, in the present context, ultraconservative regimes cancel that effect by denying youth any influence and systematically rejecting progressive ideas. Therefore, it's difficult to imagine how the formula can be imposed through economic coercion to poor countries, who will likely draw no real profit from it, especially when considering international financiers will most likely thwart any dynamic initiative to which it might lead.

A POISONED GIFT

The reason we believe electors have the right and ability to make decisions is a major criterion in deciding who votes. There are many possible approaches to this question; throughout the history of democracy, three have most often been mentioned. Each has different effects on the universality of the vote and on the nature of the system. They are as follows:

a) Electors are responsible adults, able to make thoughtful decisions about their individual and collective interests. As for personal benefits, the liberal theory concerning enlightened egotism asserts they can be trusted implicitly; their perception of the public interest is less obvious and voting procedures should logically offer the possibility of at least verifying whether citizens have the necessary information, or else the result may not be as anticipated. We saw earlier that most democracies justifiably eliminated voter-competence tests, which had often arbitrarily denied voting rights to entire classes of citizens. This no doubt explains why this rationalization of universality is hardly invoked by analysts of democracy.

b) We pretend to apply the statistical rule of large numbers, telling ourselves that everybody can't be wrong all the time and that the weaknesses, prejudices and ignorance of voters will cancel themselves out. From this we conclude that, all things being equal, the majority will be right most of the time. But this is based on two logical mistakes: first, the argument "everybody can't always be wrong," at best leads to the conclusion that the majority must be right only some of the time; second, we must realize that probability methods don't automatically correct aberrations, they only measure and quantify them, which is of no help in this case.

c) We presume leaders will be selected from a narrow list arising from a political class that selects its members on the basis of affinities and competence. As such, it doesn't really matter whom the population chooses, since the aptitude to govern was determined at a previous stage; the only role left for the vote is to stand as a last resort against dictatorship. This interpretation has become common among political scientists and is probably the most realistic. But it has two drawbacks. The first and more theoretical one is that the scope of our great democratic principles, as well as the importance of the right to vote, is thereby considerably reduced. The second, is of a more practical nature and maintains that the political class's ability to co-opt dynamic and competent people is, to say the least, challenged by recent events in countries claiming to be democratic.

Any of these explanations is very poor justification for the quasi-sacred status we confer to electoral democracy. It especially shouldn't justify twisting the arm of Third-World countries to compel them to adopt the system in the name of the "right of peoples to self-determination." In fact, the right to vote has a solid foundation only when it's acquired through struggle by succeeding groups of underprivileged citizens (middle class, workers, women, blacks) whose fortune it subsequently improves. The acquisition method is what gives it all its importance ... and the intervention of an outside force—be it the paternalism of former colonizers, American-style "gunboat diplomacy," or the UN's hypocritical human-istic sentiments—to foist it on people who neither ask for it nor know what to do with it, deprives it of value and legitimacy. If, as happens too often, it's used as an instrument of manipulation by a demagogic leader or an ambitious clique, it becomes a virtual poisoned gift and an obstacle, rather than a benefit, to the free expression of popular will.

REPRESENTATION OR PARTICIPATION

What do we vote on? According to whether popular will chooses policies, legislators, or a government team, the effects of voting differ widely. Over the last two centuries, the democratic discourse has remained ambiguous on this subject, creating a fuzziness that has been amplified by circumstances.

At the outset, the democratic system's purpose was to allow people to voice opinions on how they were governed. This happened directly in Athens (where practically all important decisions were made by public assembly), a little less in Rome, in Swiss cantons and New England town meetings, where citizens always maintained the option of intervening directly to sway representatives in desired directions. Even at the beginning of representative regimes, the existence of leaders offering clearly defined programs supported the argument that by electing a leader, the people could also choose major policy directions.

With today's ragbag and purely election-minded parties, with the multiplication of problems and the abstruse technicality of proposed solutions, with the reductive nature of electoral propaganda imposed by the electronic media's format, and abetted by opinion manipulation, that proposition is no longer relevant. In fact, comments like those of former Canadian Conservative Party leader, Kim Campbell, that "an election campaign is the worst time to discuss major issues," have become common. This explains why, after each election, experts spend months pouring over detailed results, in the vain hope of discovering "what the people meant" by its vote. Based on an assessment of major and recent issues, who would dare claim the last elections in the United States determined the right to abortion, the fate of immigrants in France, or the future of social programs in Canada.

I can therefore claim with certainty that electing representatives is all the democratic system allows us to do. Is it to legislate or to govern? Wherever both functions are treated separately (legislative and presidential elections), as in the United States and France, the situation is more clear cut; however, when conflicts between two levels of government occur, the question remains which is the most authoritative... and the answer given most often, favoring the executive, is contrary to the classical democratic doctrine that asserts the legislative branch is the highest power in the state. Imagine the confusion, then, in British-type parliamentary systems, where legislators are elected so an executive can be arbitrarily drawn from their ranks, and where they'll afterwards be completely subjected to this executive, in the name of party discipline!

It's for good reason that many authors largely blame these ambiguities for the constant decline in the political interest of citizens and for their feeling of powerlessness, which often translates into bitter scepticism. Some of them have proposed a remedy that would reduce the representative element and restore a form of direct participation into decision-making; the suggestion has come from both the American left (Carol Pateman et al.) and moderate English conservatives (Brian Beedham in "The Economist"). Unfortunately, its promoters refuse to understand it isn't only a minor adjustment to be made gradually, but rather a fundamental change in the balance of power; traditions, institutions and the mentalities of leaders and electors have been molded for generations by the representative principle. A turn-around of that magnitude would require at the very least:

a) present and future executives accepting a serious reduction in their authority and freedom of action;

b) a reduction in the influence and a restructuring of political parties;

c) an almost complete overhaul of popular consultation mechanisms, taking into account opinion polls and electronic voting techniques;

d) a redefinition of the legislature's role and the independence of representatives;

e) a reassessment of the balance between popular sovereignty and the power of courts to invalidate laws;

f) the creation or adaptation of an objective popular information service to complement and discipline state and partisan propaganda organizations.

It seems evident these changes, even spread over a long time, would inevitably produce important and perhaps brutal disturbances in our societies and especially in our ruling political class. And nothing ensures that once achieved, they'd make democracy a commodity more easily exported outside the Western-culture zone.

As we can see, whoever has a right to vote, the method and purpose of the ballot, are questions that profoundly affect the political system's equilibrium and function. Clearly, immediate circumstances can't be allowed to determine these choices, which must be guided by the public interest and civic duty as much as by personal benefit. This raises two questions: must similar rules apply in all countries, or vary according to needs and traditions; and, how can the quality of the elected be ensured?

Recent events provide a fabulously ironic answer to the first question: at the moment I write this chapter, the United Nations has disclosed its intention of favoring a restoration of the monarchy in Cambodia as the only means of achieving peace and normalcy. It matters little whether this succeeds or not. The important point is that, for the first time, the international community appears to admit that Western-style democracy is not a political panacea and that other formulas can be devised according to local problems and characteristics. The second question, which is even more complicated and vexatious, is the subject of the next chapter.

– 5 –

A POOR CHOICE
OF LEADERS

The major public media are suddenly focusing on the quality of our leaders. A uniquely virulent outbreak of this pang of conscience followed the Tokyo G-7 summit in July 1993: at a few days' interval in midsummer, displaying poignant harmony (though lagging somewhat behind the popular reaction) "Time," "Newsweek," "le Point," "le Nouvel Observateur," "Cambio 16" and others unfavorably compared the present generation of state leaders to that of the post-war era ... they were distressed, they couldn't understand. Strangely, they noted, all these leaders had been democratically elected; yet, not only were they breaking all unpopularity records, but they clearly deserved their fate. Why have all our leaders abruptly shown an innate lack of foresight, an infallible instinct for putting their feet in it?

There's nothing astonishing in this; it's simply that for the first time in over a century, democracy's fundamental mechanism is working as it should in much of the West, and we're witnessing its crude results. In fact, wars and random mishaps in each of the last five or six generations throughout states of European lineage (the 1863, 1870 and Boer wars for Europe; civil and Cuban wars in America; world wars in 1914 and 1939, political assassinations and Great Depression in 1929 nearly everywhere) thrust allegedly "providential" men into power who probably couldn't have acceded to it in more peaceful times, since they lacked the personality or "career profile" to get elected according to regular procedures: De

Gaulle, Churchill, Roosevelt, Adenauer, Pierre Elliott Trudeau ...

The prosperity and relative orderliness of the last thirty years have allowed democracy to progress normally, and demonstrated with a certain delay the truth in the observations of Aristotle (for whom it's a bad means of choosing leaders) and Tocqueville (for whom it inevitably leads to mediocrity). Minimal reflection reveals clear and obvious reasons for this: the qualities needed to be elected are, if not the opposite, then at least very different from those required to govern. We don't have the leaders we deserve; we have those allowed by the system we have adopted.

We might pretend these are temporary deviations or a series of unfortunate and random mishaps; this is the argument most often used by those who raise the problem. Alas, it doesn't withstand analysis, especially when considering not only actual leaders, but also defeated candidates and potential alternatives. We then see that leaders of most modern states aren't lamentable exceptions, but represent a solid average from the available selection, and that it's unlikely the situation will improve soon. Without providing an exhaustive demonstration, I'll only cite as examples politicians in France, Canada and the United States at the beginning of the 1990s. Who would dare say, in each of those cases, that a different electoral result in the last decade would have enhanced the quality of leaders ... or that we can expect a clear improvement in the next ten years?

While Athenian democracy considered the selection of leaders as secondary to the determination of social policy, our system is elective: it's used almost exclusively to select leaders. A biblical proverb says that "a tree is known by its fruit;" similarly, our democracy must be judged primarily by the quality of people it carries to power. In that respect, results haven't been convincing, to say the least: some elected leaders are dishonest and brazenly profit from their office, others clearly don't have the expertise needed to fulfill their mandate and, finally, most don't seem to have the intellectual rigor nor moral fibre needed to choose and implement policies that are difficult and unpopular, but essential to public interest.

It's paradoxical that we deplore the poor quality of leaders, without openly challenging the selection mechanism designed almost exclusively to elect them. Yet, it's easy to demonstrate that some of the system's characteristics are directly responsible for this situation. Among these factors: the impossibility of setting objective candidate-qualification criteria, the electoral system's emphasis on image and personality, the role of political parties and the rather clandestine filtering of future representatives. Add to these, recent and serious doubts about the political class's ability to confront the new demands of economic evolution and of society generally.

EXPERTISE AND COMMON SENSE

According to the logic of representative democracy, the minimum official requirements for becoming President of the United States or British Prime Minister are (and must be) essentially the same as for having the right to vote. Most countries add minor criteria such as age limits, the absence of a criminal record in some cases, and proof of property ownership. To prevent any appearance of favoritism or injustice, eligibility conditions that explicitly insist on competence or integrity are avoided. As a result, the more a system is democratic, the more it's likely to produce incompetent or dishonest leaders. But the absence of real proficiency criteria is essential to prove to the population that the contest is really open, that all citizens are on an equal footing. Anyhow, the imposition of candidate tests or exams would probably run into the same problems as it does for electors, and lead to the same dangers of discrimination and despotism mentioned in the previous chapter.

This defect, however, ensures that criteria for heads of state are lower than those for doctors or chartered accountants. We rely on the intelligence of citizens to choose leaders able to make decisions of which we judge the public is unable. This is somewhat like asking unskilled jurors to grant professional-competence certificates in disciplines foreign to them: could a surgeon or administrator who had acquired the right to practice his profession in this way be trusted? The paradox is that a government controls the health and fate, not of a limited number of clients, but of an entire population.

Throughout much of liberal-democratic history, being an educated bourgeois, adequately informed about laws and events was a sufficient qualification for leading a government. The moderate tempo of evolution, the predominance of the mechanical-manufacturing industry in the economy, the modest technicality of options and decisions, made this minimal competence level acceptable, as long as it was accompanied by a good measure of common sense and civic responsibility. Major policies were determined on this basis; details were left to bureaucrats having greater professional expertise.

These criteria still apply throughout Western countries ... but are no longer adequate. As our societies become more complex and less homogeneous, as we evolve from an industrial and commercial economy to one of information, as the government is transformed into a huge and sophisticated data-processing device, the knowledge needed to simply understand problems becomes more extensive and specific. Systems theory teaches us the more an organism is complex, the more powerful it is ... but it's also more fragile and likely to break down as a result of the tiniest mechanical flaw; this relates to the theory of chaos. In such circumstances, planning must be more detailed and long-term, and its directives more specific. As well, decisions have much more serious results. The political class created by traditional middle-class elites only suits those new requirements occasionally, and the constant dependence on hired specialists becomes an unacceptable constraint.

It's no accident that individuals with economics and administration backgrounds hold power in a growing number of governments. This tendency is explained, albeit imperfectly, by the new need for expertise at the highest levels. Another approach has been taken, notably in the United States, with the creation of management teams; these can be either hidden, such as the one behind Ronald Reagan, or public like the one headed by Bill Clinton, his wife Hillary, and his vice-president, Al Gore. This need for professionalism is also felt on a smaller scale. Many North-American cities are no longer run by an elected mayor, but by a salaried municipal administrator. Popular control is ensured by elected municipal councils, whose function resembles that of a company's board of directors, before whom the manager is publicly responsible.

When does the usual selection mechanism of our liberal democracies allow the transition to governments having the technical expertise that is increasingly necessary? The unpredictable nature of the elective system doesn't allow the efficient training of men and women needed to fill the most important public-administration positions. Plain common sense remains necessary, but is no longer an adequate basis for decision (no more than it can be in any discipline that's very technical, such as brain surgery or nuclear physics).

POPULARITY OR COMPETENCE

A second part of the problem is the traditional nature of elections as popularity contests, which has been accentuated over the last two or three decades by the pervasiveness of the electronic media. Nothing illustrates this better than an example; that of Ronald Reagan in the United States is likely the most obvious and comprehensive one in recent history, especially with the new light shed by subsequent revelations from his immediate entourage.

A second-rate actor specializing in action films and television advertising, then reborn as a politician, Reagan had, in the highest degree, the looks, voice and behavior needed to be elected. He fit the stereotype of the straightforward conservative "grand-dad" in almost all points; according to polls and studies, this is what American electors wanted following the shocks of Richard Nixon's Watergate deviousness, and

Jimmy Carter's amateurish liberalism. As well, his numerous film roles as a cowboy or military hero gave him an aura of firmness and decisiveness that could only please a population traumatized by the humiliating Vietnam defeat. His record as California governor, at a time when the state underwent exceptional growth and minimal problems, provided him a reputation as a competent administrator. Finally, his near-complete lack of ideological conviction and coherent views (save for a more sentimental that reasoned penchant for the right) made him a malleable substance on which image-makers could exercise their skill to perfection.

He was elected twice with imposing majorities, without his aptitude to govern ever being seriously challenged. Moreover, his reign was a gigantic media spectacle hardly tarnished by the few incidents that raised doubts about his capacity to understand and confront problems: the admission he napped during cabinet meetings, his difficulty understanding any slightly complicated question raised by journalists, gross errors of fact in extemporaneous statements—the most flagrant happening when Corazon Aquino was elected in the Philippines. We now know what we only suspected then: to all practical purposes, Ronald Reagan didn't govern. He was the spokesman and figurehead of an ultraconservative "political team" that analyzed situations, determined strategies and simply submitted pre-arranged decisions for his approval, in terms any ten-year old could understand. His real purpose was to disseminate through the population messages whose content came from elsewhere and whose form was devised with the help of "spin doctors," image and slogan makers.

Despite this, and sometimes because of it, many American and even foreign experts considered his presidency a success. Several claim that, given the complexity and technicality of today's problems, such a division of tasks will ensure the best results and will likely become widespread. They forget two of its serious drawbacks. First, the major decision-making criterion is neither the soundness nor the effectiveness of a solution, but its "saleability" to the population. Second, the state, or at least the government, is in the hands of people who are neither elected, nor responsible to elected members, which is contrary to the foundations of the democratic ideal. The obvious conclusion is that popularity alone is a very poor criterion for the selection of leaders, if they are to display a genuine ability to govern.

CIVIC CONSCIENCE VS. PRIVATE INTEREST

In the city-states of antiquity, the right of appointment to public office often depended on proof of devotion to the state, provided among other things by a family tradition of public service or by military feats. This idea (though evident among the American Constitution's Founding Fathers and at the French Convention) has been almost completely removed from modern democracies, which have no requirements concerning this crucial point. The only restrictions designed to limit the risks of personal ambition, collusion or dishonesty are applied after, instead of before, the election; for example, there's an obligation in North America to disclose real estate and stock portfolios, or even to sell or place in a blind trust any investments that might lead to conflicts of interest.

Yet, the integrity of public figures is becoming more important for electoral systems governing industrial states. Economic decisions have serious repercussions that can affect the future of important companies, ready to spend huge sums to ensure the benevolence of political leaders. The bigger the stakes, the greater the temptation. The electoral mechanism forces candidates to solicit funds as much from corporations (or labor unions) as from individuals. In many cases, fund raisers consider that "electoral debts" must be repaid, notably through privileged access to decision makers or a transfer of confidential information. These dealings were once discreet and informal; they've now become almost public through lobbying and fund-raising events where guests are guaranteed access to one or more ministers, in exchange for a monetary contribution. Another aspect of the same problem concerns the rewards awaiting public figures when they return to private life; they're immediately offered highly paid and important positions with companies. This system has increasingly replaced under-the-table kickbacks, which are riskier and easier to trace; although it's technically legal, it can exert the same undue influence on political decisions, before and after the fact. However, very few countries have adopted rules forbidding or circumscribing that type of behavior.

It certainly isn't easy to devise practical methods to preserve the independence of public men against external pressures. Plato, who was likely the first to address the problem, proposed a radical solution: impose a communist-type system on the political class, allowing it neither property nor money, but with sumptuous comfort guaranteed by the state. This closely resembled the Soviet system's privileges of office (luxury apartments, special stores, choice medical clinics) provided government and party leaders. It remains to be seen which approach, between the leash of more or less rugged democratic rules or the sausage collar of Plato and the Kremlin, is more likely to hold the dogs properly!

THE TRAP OF PRIMARIES

The most democratically logical solution to this dilemma was devised in America because, among other things, the first parties that were purely election-minded appeared in the United States: it was the least stratified Western society and it was normal for parties to have no definite ideology. This led to the rise of local potentates (ward bosses) who controlled and manipulated captive electorates whom they literally sold to one politician or another; these "kingmakers" then confederated to choose and place their men in the most lucrative positions. Primaries were introduced to counter this appropriation of the electoral mechanism by a clique of "back-room boys." Today, this formula seems to fascinate many other countries.

The basic idea is simple and outwardly convincing: spread the responsibility of electors upwards by allowing them to choose not only representatives, but candidates as well. The formula varies from one region to the next; sometimes all voters are consulted, and other times only members of a given party. Sometimes the choice is direct, sometimes delegates are selected who must vote according to their electors' wishes. A few decades were required to achieve the desired result. The first presidential candidate rejected by the establishment, but supported by the grass roots, was likely the very conservative Barry Goldwater in 1964; the first president elected in this way was the liberal Jimmy Carter in 1976, the last, Bill Clinton in 1992.

If the mechanism helped wrest selection control from furtive manipulators, it nonetheless has important and disturbing side effects:

a) It places emphasis on image and personal popularity, at the expense of ideas and program coherence, even earlier in the process.

b) It gives free rein to pressure groups pursuing narrow and specific ends, either to impose their choice or effectively block any candidate not ready to give in to their demands.

c) It short-circuits any possibility of applying minimal competence and honesty criteria inside political parties for the pre-selection of representatives.

d) It prolongs election campaigns beyond the limits of what is bearable, over nearly an entire year, causing perceptible disaffection among electors with respect to their political responsibilities.

These conclusions are drawn from the comments of principal political analysts and from a summary study of a list of successful and defeated candidates during the last two decades. As it turns out, eccentrics and marginals who've fallen along the way would have been weeded out by any other method. Besides, the most prominent victims of the "obstacle course" of the primaries have been politicians who demonstrated clarity and resolve in their political vision, and those who appealed to the intelligence and judgment of citizens rather than to their passions. Major winners were often those best at exploiting emotions and manipulating the media, notably by relying on the most militant and vociferous minorities.

Can we say the same about any other type of election campaign? If so, we must consider whether results are those we want from a leadership-selection process; this challenges the merits of a mechanism that increases costs and duration to arrive at the same point and, ultimately, the concept of a campaign as we know it. If not, we're forced to admit that primaries may very well distort the entire process. Either way, we conclude that entrusting the entire electorate, or members of a political party, with the responsibility of validating candidacies to public office, doesn't solve the crucial problem of leadership competence; on the contrary.

INFORMAL FILTERS

To obviate the flagrant absence of an official mechanism for the qualification of future elected members, other than the dubious technique of primaries, most representative systems have devised a variety of methods to screen candidates. The only feature common to all these informal filters is their fundamentally undemocratic nature which mostly rests on privileged personal relationships between political leaders, and on the hierarchical functioning of the party apparatus. As for the rest, variations can be attributed to conditions such as the type of state (centralized or federal), the size and make-up of political and economic elites, the role and importance of public institutions, etc.

These techniques aren't mutually exclusive; they frequently intermingle or are used differently by rival political groups in the same country. I'll stick to the following narrow list and brief description; my goal isn't to analyze this phenomenon exhaustively, but only to demonstrate its existence and highlight its main features.

CO-OPTATION

In this case, the political class chooses new members on the basis of personal ties, regardless of ideological or party differences, most often by using aristocratic criteria. Traces of such an attitude are found in most Western democracies, but the purest and oldest example is the very British "old boys" institution.

It isn't only that the great majority of English leaders are from noble or upper-class families (the "gentry"), nor even that they attended the same exclusive and famous public schools. Mostly, it's because they nearly all knew each other in their youth and have maintained, regardless of political differences, private relationships that weave a virtual network that transcends party barriers. For example, party leaders often secretly consult their opponents before naming one of their members to an important position or, conversely, leaders of the opposition intervene discreetly, and successfully, to block a government nomination they feel is inappropriate.

MAJOR SCHOOLS

Another method is to guarantee basic technical training through a quasi-mandatory attendance at certain institutions. Evidence of this is found in England with the preponderance of graduates from Eton, Harrow, or Rugby; but it's applied most systematically in France, where nearly all political leaders attended the state's "Grandes Écoles," the main one being the ÉNA (École nationale d'administration), followed by Saint-Cyr (military and combined arms), Polytechnique (military and civil engineering) and the Nationale supérieure (higher-level teachers).

There's obviously no formal obligation in this regard, but a rapid overview of prominent politicians reveals a clear preponderance of "énarques" (ÉNA graduates) and a very low proportion of leaders who aren't from a major school:

former socialist Prime Ministers Pierre Mauroy and Pierre Bérégovoy were notable exceptions to this rule.

The obvious advantage is that it ensures future leaders can be culled from a political class, most of whose members have already acquired intellectual rigor and a knowledge of the state. The drawback is the quasi-confidential nature of the process, with its overtones of favoritism and influence peddling, given the difficulty of access to major schools and the arbitrariness of the subsequent selection.

STRUCTURE

Another approach requires that a leader demonstrate competence at a subordinate level before acceding to the higher ranks of power. It's displayed in two distinct forms: in federal-type systems, where the skill to govern is acquired locally or regionally before being recognized nationally, and within party structures (often with ideological predominance) where it's a function of the ability to climb the hierarchy's echelons one at a time.

The most extreme example of the first form is found in Germany, where leaders of regional states (Lander) are naturally given ministerial positions. But it's also applied less formally and systematically in other federations like the United States, Canada and Brazil. The second form prevails in many socialist parties and, more generally, in popular blocs organized in a pyramidal structure.

Such an approach obviously perpetuates the reigning oligarchy by offering it a rational method of co-opting new members, within the favorable environment of its own partisans. On the other hand, it often leads to dubious results that confirm the Peter principle: it's not because an apparatchik has displayed efficiency as a subordinate that he can be a high-level leader.

WEALTH EQUALS COMPETENCE

The oldest and most popular informal filter likens the capacity of running a private business to that of administering a state. It was already found in the United States and England nearly two centuries ago; after a long hiatus, it surfaced again with the 1980s conservative wave, that measured all forms of competence against financial success and asserted that the state, in the scarce areas it was thought to have a role, ought to function like a private business.

Curiously, experience provides almost daily refutation of this claim. Most often, businessmen who've entered politics experience moderate success at best, while former politicians often become competent corporate managers. This is likely because the former underestimate the complexity of problems confronting state administrations, while the latter, suddenly freed from the multiple constraints and responsibilities of public life, have elbow room to give free rein to the initiative and decisiveness they whetted in the political arena. Yet, the myth of "good managers" from the private sector is astonishingly difficult to dispel, especially in Canada and the United States.

THE EFFECT OF POLITICAL PARTIES

Democracy's original principles didn't include political parties; indeed, factions were mistrusted in the Greek and Roman systems, where mechanisms had been devised to either prevent their creation or reduce their influence. But the appearance of the first popular-suffrage systems in the United States, France and England at the turn of the 19th century was almost immediately followed by the creation of relatively durable political blocs, as though that had been an unavoidable consequence.

The first definition of party was basically ideological: it was in Burke's famous words a "body of men united for promoting by their joint endeavors the national interest upon some particular principle in which they are all agreed." Marx and his successors refined this definition by adding that parties each represent and defend a social class. This image is preserved by electoral programs and organization names: Socialists, Labour, Christian-Democrats, Conservatives ... In practice, however, parties have mostly become mechanisms that finance campaigns and elect candidates. They have no great cohesion in the realm of ideas; good examples are the recent evolution of the French Socialist Party and the interchangeability of the two major American parties. Defenders of the modern representative system argue that political parties are essential to the democratic process in large states. They are necessary because the size and dispersion of the population prevent voters from getting directly acquainted with candidates. As well, the high cost of campaigns would otherwise allow only wealthy individuals (or those supported by them) to run for office. Accepting this argument means accepting the necessity of political parties as well as understanding they have an unavoidable effect on voting. We therefore face three possibilities: a single, double or multiparty system. The liberal model rejects the first hypothesis— although that rejection is much less categorical in practice, as we'll see further on.

Let's begin with bipartisan government, which is often linked to British parliamentary tradition where the executive is directly drawn from the legislature, the notable exception being the United States, which adapts it to a presidential system. This formula seemingly responds to a natural cleavage: conservative-progressive, tradition-change, left-right. It almost guarantees a somewhat regular alternation between the two tendencies, and provides each with a positive role in the mechanism: they form a complementary couple whose "brake-accelerator" system allows a nation periods of rapid sociopolitical and economic evolution, followed by a calmer period of digestion and adjustment to change. Taking turns in opposition provides parties with a critical view of the country's government and time to renew themselves to return to power with fresh troops and new ideas.

However, this system has flaws. First, it doesn't permit a varied range of ideological or strategic choices, but reduces everything to two main premises that are too cut-and-dried and simplistic for the richness and variety of human opinions. Second, it creates governments having absolute power during their mandates, generating a type of "dictatorship of the majority," where minorities have no political mechanism to protect their interests; this almost necessarily leads to the systematic and sometimes abusive use of legal procedures and the need for a suprapolitical arbitrator (Supreme or Constitutional Court) that is most often appointed and therefore of a non-democratic nature.

The multiparty approach, which is most prevalent in Continental Europe and areas of the world that have felt its influence, favors the expression of a greater variety of ideological options, not only in the classical range of left-center-right, but also for the defence of specific causes ("Greens", antinuclear activists), or ethnic or regional interests. It most often leads to coalition governments that can only survive by establishing and maintaining the largest possible consensus. As such, it provides much greater minority rights protection than bipartisan government; the proof is that court intervention isn't required as often to invalidate or "correct" measures adopted by legislatures.

The flip side of the coin is that such governments are frequently unstable and have short life spans; they tend to temporarily juxtapose parties whose agreement on major issues is superficial, not to say exclusively tactical. The result is a lack of coherence, an absence of guidelines and sometimes even a dangerous paralysis. Finally, regional blocs having no national scope emerge, especially in federal-type states, and threaten to warp the entire process or even precipitate the country's dislocation. That's presently the case, for example, in Canada and Italy.

The complementary qualities or defects of these two approaches likely caused a curious phenomenon that arose over the last two decades: while bipartisan countries tend to drift towards a multiplication of parties, those already in that state experience the opposite effect as their great coalitions, at first temporary, congeal into left and right-wing blocs, where the identity of constituents becomes much less perceptible. At the time this is written, Canada and France are the most obvious theatres of this inversion of traditions: the latter now only reasons in terms of power and opposition, while the former heads towards a five-party Parliament (with two regional factions) where traditional alignments between left and right are significantly blurred.

The United States has until now escaped this movement. Its two major parties seem relatively unthreatened by splits or third candidates coming up the middle, despite the emergence of Ross Perot in 1992. The simplest explanation is the American system only appears to be bipartisan. It functions almost like a single-party system whose point of equilibrium is located on the center-right of the ideological scale.

When looking beyond electoral rhetoric and slogans tailored to create an impression of substantial differences and cater to the tastes of rather distinct clienteles, Republicans and Democrats appear to have many more similarities than differences. Both are openly Christian, liberal, republican, capitalist and individualist, and share a minimalist view of government. Moreover, their personnel and electorates are largely interchangeable, and their representatives, being free from party discipline and ideological constraints, regularly form ad hoc alliances with their opponents on a regional, moral or tactical basis. For example, it's common in some regions of the country that Democrats are on "the left" (as far as that's possible in the USA), while in others it's the Republicans.

All told, the American elector, as in a single-party system, doesn't have a choice between two or more views, nor between government teams—since there's no party discipline and the executive isn't drawn from the legislature—but only between individuals. The long prohibition of genuine left or right-wing parties and the extreme economic and legal difficulties of breaking the closed circle, tend to perpetuate this de facto single-party system without its existence ever being admitted openly.

Is a genuine elective democracy possible in a single-party context? Nothing prevents it in theory, as long as the citizen has a real choice between various candidates. Otherwise, we'd either have to conclude the United States isn't a democratic state, or that its system is founded on a bipartisan fiction. Besides, there are a number of examples (albeit limited) of "national unity" single parties that function rather well in this respect. On the other hand, so-called popular republics that have adopted dictatorship of the proletariat, and the numerous countries where single parties serve only as a pretext for maintaining a "strong man" or a restricted clique in power, are far from the Franco-American model and the Lincolnian ideal of government "of the people, by the people and for the people." Therefore, they can't be called democracies according to the most current definition.

In conclusion, political parties are very rarely democratic power structures, either in liberal states or other systems; even when they are, the competence and integrity of representatives aren't ensured in the least, save through use of mostly unacknowledged "informal filters." Moreover, the power they've acquired as essential parts of the electoral mechanism makes them natural opponents of any shift towards a more direct form of participatory democracy.

-6-

WARRING BROTHERS

Democracy was virtually born at the same time as industrial capitalism. Was this only a coincidence, or is there a link between the two? The first to establish this connection precisely was Karl Marx. He underlined that the bourgeoisie, whose ascent was primarily due to capitalism, was the social class that virtually imposed democracy as the political system that best responded to its needs; a majority of historians, even the most liberal, today agree with him.

Our study of the social contract's nature and the historical context confirms this, but also strongly suggests the phenomenon is more complex than a mere causal relation. There is an adversarial relation between liberal democracy and capitalism that makes them warring brothers. There's a conflict between the state's role as an administrator and distributor of collective wealth, and that of non-interference in the economy required by the free-market approach ... which, however, couldn't function effectively without the stability and justice offered by the "rule of law."

A fascinating chapter in the history of political thought, particularly during the second half of the 19th century in England and the United States, features attempts to reconcile the philosophical and political liberalism of John Stuart Mill, and his successors, with the commercial and industrial liberalism conceived by Adam Smith. The appearance of trade-unionism was especially useful in revealing that the word "liberalism" concealed two very dissimilar notions: political freedoms are completely different from laissez-faire economics, and the equality of citizens' rights doesn't translate into equality of work or income. This logical and practical difficulty has only been overcome by rather imperfect compromises between both doctrines.

Nowadays, it's considered increasingly necessary for the state's role in the economy to be a function of the minimalist requirements of classical economic theory, rather than social options determined on a much broader basis by each state. Economic liberalism clearly prevails over its political counterpart. It's rather ironic that while Western regimes managed to discredit communism as a form of government, they have more and more openly adopted one of its fundamental premises: democratic systems exclusively favor the interests of the propertied class, whose benefit is likened to the country's welfare; renaming this doctrine "supply-side" economics and presuming it creates collective wealth in the long term ("the trickle-down effect") changes nothing to its reality, which Marx would have recognized at first glance.

I have no intention of providing a historical account or detailed analysis of this relation, but the subject must be broached briefly for two reasons. First, the dominant ideology advocates democracy and capitalism, as though they went hand in hand; it therefore pretends to export both realities throughout the world … as well as the paradox and disputes opposing them. Second, governing requires foresight and planning; however, the doctrine of free-market omnipotence on the one hand, and electoral necessities on the other, create serious obstacles to any long-term planning.

A FORMULA ALMOST MADE TO MEASURE

It's difficult for Westerners to imagine a world where money isn't perceived as power in itself. Yet, this was the case for us during thousands of years, and it's still so for people throughout much of the world. For them, capital is neither the cause nor the equivalent of power, but only its manifestation. As long as it was considered as such—as a simple means of exchange or precious metal—in Europe, there was no use hoarding it, and it could only be spent. For example, Christianity and Islam forbade their followers from exacting interest from one another and therefore making a direct profit from the ownership of money (which in passing explains how Jews became, almost by default, the bankers of these two civilizations!). To generate a real profit, it had to be transformed into land or armed forces.

In this context, the middle class—which drew profits from industry, lived in cities and owned no great estates—couldn't assert itself against the land-owning and military aristocracy. It's only during the Renaissance, with the emergence of Lombard financiers and new tools for managing money (banks, shares, stock exchanges) that control of the transformation of goods through labor began to translate into real power. The first solid examples were the British and Flemish textile industries. However, an ingredient for the rapid increase of wealth was still missing: it was provided by the technical and scientific progress that occurred between the 16th and 19th centuries, that propagated machines capable of increasing human effort, while reducing the strength and ability needed from each worker.

However, for this newborn capitalism to perform at its best, certain conditions had to combine: stable currencies, moderate and predictable tax and duty rates, solid protection of private property, particularly in its new and volatile form as paper capital, freedom of action and movement for manufacturers and merchants, as well as for their goods. The monarchical systems of the time were whimsical and despotic, profligate and bellicose, sustained by an aristocracy disdainful of trade and hoarding; they obviously didn't respond to those needs. This explains the bourgeoisie's attraction, first to constitutional monarchy, and then to republican democracy.

The system finally adopted transcended basic economic necessity, for various reasons: to subdue the monarchy, the middle class needed the support of the popular mass and therefore had to grant it certain concessions; moreover, it perceived itself as the incarnation of what was foremost in the people, and of a higher morality (that of work, equality of opportunity, the sacrosanct status of the individual ...) it wanted to transplant into the political system; it finally had to consider the broader necessities of the social contract and the state's traditional role. Therefore, many of the system's characteristics were either tailor made for the smooth operation of industry and commerce, or greatly beneficial to it.

THE STATE AS ECONOMIC AGENT

The doctrine advocating primacy of the market was first contrived by French physiocrats during the mid-18th century, in the name of respect for "natural law." Its definitive formulation was conceived by Adam Smith, the founder of modern economics. When it appeared, it wasn't so much opposed to economic planning as to mercantilism, a theory maintaining that a country's wealth is measured in precious metals, and that it should therefore promote any means for acquiring them, and discourage anything leading to their export. This required government intervention in trade and industry, a form of protectionism prevalent during the 17th and 18th centuries in England and France (notably in the cases of Sully and Colbert). On the other hand, economic liberalism maintained that, left alone, the market would self-regulate and create wealth while providing the population with the best goods at the best prices.

For this, commercial operations had to occur exclusively in the private sector, with practically no interference from the state, whose weight and power threatened to warp the mechanism. Yet, this theory implied conditions and operating rules that applied to all: currency stability and reliability, protection of private property, freedom of movement for people and goods inside and outside the country, prohibition of fraud and monopolies, etc. Only public authority could provide such a framework, and it therefore remained prominent in the market, at least as an arbiter. This regulatory function is essential in any liberal system; only the extent to which it must apply to economic activity remains to be determined. The least thinking on this reveals there is no single and absolute answer; the choice depends on each nation, according to its circumstances, needs and traditions.

Add to this first paradox that the state, by its very nature, has a direct role in the economy. How else could it administer the public responsibilities which the community confers to it? Most attempts to contract these affairs out to private interests have shown that solution to be not only unjust but, paradoxically, inefficient. It's striking that individuals who condemn public intervention in their businesses are the first to accuse governments of being poor administrators and accumulating deficits. While they oppose state planning and subsidies in principle, they hasten to use public funds and demand government action when their affairs turn awry. But when the state acts in the name of public interest (which often coincides with the benefit of a group of proprietors) to save or help a private company with public funds, strict justice would require that this rather furtive capitalization be rewarded as it would in a private transaction with a proportional stake in property and decision-making power; which inevitably leads to state capitalism.

SHARED ASSETS OR COMMONWEALTH

The key role of governments in managing public resources for the benefit of all, is implied in the definition of "social contract," and explicitly written in the constitutions of numerous countries. As such, despite claims by the oracles of unequivocal liberalism, the state has an essential economic role, other than that of a mere arbiter responsible for the market's smooth running.

First, the private property concept underlying European liberalism is much less "natural" than believed by its first proponents who, to justify the idea, relied mostly on the division of land into individual lots. However, ownership of property was foreign to many societies that lived from hunting and raising livestock; their lifestyle was basically nomadic and various communities took turns inhabiting the same land in different seasons. Pastures, forests and some fields often remained communal and undivided property, even after the appearance of agriculture. Today, property titles and land registries, which are so firmly rooted in the European mentality, remain vague or unknown concepts in many countries: the land belongs to a peasant as long as he cultivates it; but, if he has to leave it for whatever reason, he would never think of selling it.

In many cases, when a primitive society becomes a state, the latter takes charge of administering land and other property considered as belonging to everybody. It should be noted that the English term "commonwealth," before it acquired its present specialized definition, had the double meaning of "common good," both literally (physical property) and figuratively (well-being). Even in the most capitalist societies, the state owns on behalf of the public, either directly or through the intervention of private entrepreneurs, a great deal of property that includes: the undersoil and its minerals, waterways, ocean and sea coasts, public buildings and parks, airways, the electromagnetic spectrum, roads, military arsenals, currency, etc. The list varies from one country to the next according to tradition, as well as the requirements of economic and political evolution. However, it always implies a more complex and refined administrative mechanism than in the private sector, since there is a tendency to demand a higher level of precision and responsibility for managing public funds and property.

DISTRIBUTION OF WEALTH

The state must also ensure a reasonable distribution of wealth among citizens, especially in democracies and systems where leaders need popular support. Citizens basically expect that the government to which they yielded their political rights guarantees them at least the possibility of satisfying their hunger (a textbook case probably being the Baa'thi dictator-

ship in Iraq during the 1970s and 1980s, where this phenomenon was very evident). Sometimes this is done out of fear of
revolution, sometimes through the influence of unions and
other popular movements, and sometimes even through the
relatively spontaneous action of an enlightened despotism, as
in Bismarck's Germany.

The issue isn't only one of morality or justice; eminently
practical reasons can be found, in terms of security, domestic
order and the stability of commerce. For example, in a
consumer society, efforts must be made to ensure a high
percentage of the population isn't forced into a parallel
underground economy. It's usually less expensive, in a context of abundance, to provide everyone with a minimum than
to fund a system that maintains order through terror: the cost
of one police officer is equivalent to that of many welfare
recipients. The recent evolution of American society (urban
violence, social unrest, drug trafficking ...) provides a convincing example.

Unfortunately, in many countries, this easily justifiable and
basic principle is obscured by a plethora of complex and
specialized programs created by electioneering concerns or
specific circumstances that have lost their relevance. Social
security, unemployment insurance, family allowances, progressive taxes and other similar measures often overlap and
contradict each other, adding to the search for a relative
equalization of revenues, that of other unrelated results
(demographic growth or stabilization, increased state revenues, protection against job losses) that were originally
temporary but usually become permanent.

In a capitalist system, the need for justice must be balanced
against the maintenance of inequalities that are essential to
the creation of capital goods. If the rich are needed to provide
investment, the condition of the poor must not be allowed to
deteriorate to the point they have nothing to spend or are ready
to rebel violently. Governments must maintain a fragile and
changing equilibrium between the two objectives, which are
threatened by excessively ideological left and right-wing

attitudes. Both sides fight in the name of opposing concepts of morality ("no handouts to the idle" on one side, and "justice for the needy" on the other) without realizing that the real forces at play are political and economic.

THE STATE AS ECONOMIC MAINSPRING

Practically no poor country has become wealthy under a democratic system in the modern era. However, such cases are to be found in oligarchies or even the most repressive tyrannies, not to mention people's republics (Singapore, Chile and Hungary are recent examples of each type). The electoral model doesn't favor the unpopular decisions often needed for rapid economic growth. This little-known but important aspect of the adversarial relation between capitalism and democracy has to be highlighted ... and explained more specifically to inhabitants of the Third World, to whom we are trying to sell the democratic formula.

Underdeveloped countries generally don't have the infrastructure and private capital allowing them to depend exclusively on the free market. Unable to withstand the brutal competition from advanced economies, they are most often vassalized to foreign powers (public or private) that exploit their labor and resources to the limit, appropriating all profits and leaving practically nothing behind. The rare exceptions are nearly all nations that use their only real strength, that of the state, as a mainspring for development. They close their markets to the invasion of foreign goods—rather completely and for a relatively long time—until they reach a size and stability that enable them to face outside competition.

EXCESSIVE SIMPLIFICATION

Let's accept for the sake of argument that man is a "complex of needs," as Marx claimed, and that those needs are exclusively material. It doesn't follow automatically that they all can be satisfied in the economic sphere or by the free market. Among the four basic needs of life that are generally accepted—food, shelter, reproduction, physical security—only the first two can be satisfied through organized work. The other two derive from social structures. On the one hand, society offers an environment that provides an adequate supply of sexual partners, and on the other, a mechanism that ensures protection from external threats, as well as from despotism and the excessive use of force on the domestic front.

This implies that, in addition to a politically dominant class needed to harmonize the production of food and build communities, the army, police and courts (the latter both to settle disputes and regulate registries) are intrinsic to human institutions in one form or another, regardless of economic evolution. These functions may once have been filled jointly by the same authorities, but it's obvious they respond to fundamental and specific human needs. Needs for which men haven't devised individual solutions ... and to which collective labor isn't the answer either.

Accordingly, whatever system we live under, bringing everything down to economics, as we're doing, is a serious error. The simplifications of Adam Smith and Karl Marx were certainly useful in explaining some previously unknown aspects of society's dynamics. However, since they were only simplifications, they shouldn't be mistaken for comprehensive models. Not only do they ignore essential aspects of the state's role, but they completely disregard the inevitable battles between the assumptions of economic and political liberalism.

These points of friction are already numerous. For example: the conflict between management rights and labor's freedom of association; the opposition between the global free market and the sovereignty of nations; between public and private schools; free competition and consumer protection; freedom of information and the right to privacy; taxation and the freedom of capital; the need for social programs and the reduction of fiscal burdens, etc.

These conflicts are spiraling as the tools we devise allow individuals or companies a greater influence on their surroundings. The most striking example is pollution, since responsibility for it is diffuse and much of the problem transcends national borders. Three different approaches have been suggested. They're based on three opposing viewpoints that correspond to distinct political concepts: local and international regulation, compensation of victims through a judicial mechanism and a self-regulating economically based system. Nothing demonstrates the internal contradictions of liberal thought better than this confusion.

Two aspects of the democracy-capitalism relation are of specific interest to us. The first is ascertaining whether it's possible to have one without the other. If we refer to Western-style liberal democracy, the answer is probably no, for the following reason: as far as we know, only capitalism can generate a prosperous middle class. Moreover, that class is the only one which demonstrates a need and ability to impose the combination of stability and freedom of action that democracy provides to those who profit from it. An aristocracy or plutocracy doesn't need popular suffrage to ensure these characteristics; a popular mass will justifiably favor security and material well-being over freedom and, save in cases of exceptional prosperity, it will tend to accept more readily an authoritarian government without concern for its legitimacy, as long as it satisfies those basic needs.

The second question, to be examined more closely in the next chapter, concerns the foresight and planning increasingly needed to succeed and govern. The quasi-blind faith in the merits of the free market and prevention of the state from intervening actively in the economy are characteristics of classical capitalism that produce obstacles which are difficult to avoid. The United States and the United Kingdom have virulently denounced communism's state planning; they refuse to entertain that many of their liberal allies (Japan and Germany more specifically) rather discreetly practice another kind of planning that is more flexible and based on consensus, which provides them a clear advantage on international markets. Washington has only recently, and timidly, begun to consider the possibility of long-term industrial policy that would link the business world and the state.

-7-

THE PROCRUSTEAN
ELECTORAL BED

Governing requires foresight. Although this principle is often mentioned, it's seldom applied in modern states. But it remains totally relevant, both in the long and short-term. On the one hand, meticulous planning that stretches over a decade or more is needed to address the size and complexity of contemporary endeavors; on the other, the acceleration of events demands an ability to change direction rapidly, even for the major policies of a state. That in itself is nothing new. What is new, is the increased urgency prompted by the appearance of the "information society," which is created by advanced technologies in data transmission and manipulation.

The two following observations may therefore be drawn: everything in the world is occurring more rapidly; and everything has a greater span in time and space. However, tight electoral deadlines in our style of democracy create a renewal period for mandates and leaders that is too long for the first and too brief for the second. Moreover, seeking popularity at all costs to be elected dangerously restricts the acuity, objectivity and breadth of vision of leaders, while the liberal doctrine's narrow restrictions on state involvement practically eliminate their room to maneuver. Finally, although alternation of power is a healthy practice, its recent avatars threaten even the best conceived plans at each change of government.

Much of the recent social and financial crisis throughout the West is likely due to this situation. It's difficult to imagine how we can prevent it from continuing or recurring.

THE LONG AND SHORT-TERM

The renewal cycle of elected governments and leaders varies according to country, from two years (United States Congress) to seven years (the French presidency). In parliamentary systems, where this process has no set timetable, custom usually schedules it every four or five years. The nature and duration of those mandates were formerly directly linked to the state's geography, as we can imagine, and to available communication methods. Political science, which usually considers governments as power structures, often forgets they are also mechanisms for gathering, processing and storing important quantities of administrative and demographic data. Foresight requires knowledge. It's no coincidence that all vast empires on all continents mastered some form of writing and calculation, nor that they created and used the most advanced means of communication available in their time.

The modest size of Greek city-states allowed a majority of citizens to be rapidly consulted. It was therefore logical for decisions to be made collectively and for people to be named to authoritative positions very briefly; however, a lack of rapid and dependable means of communication prompted Hellenic colonies founded on the edge of the Mediterranean to become autonomous and even rival, instead of coalescing into an empire. As long as Rome remained a rather modest city, it maintained the same kind of mechanism; as soon as it became the hub of a vast empire, it had to devise new solutions on two fronts. It gradually extended the mandates of its leaders, going to the extreme of granting them power for life, and designed a communication system that was very advanced for its time: construction of an effective navy, and a network of highways scoured by messengers through a sophisticated relay system, that allowed rapid communication and intervention. Corresponding observations could be made about other empires such as China and the Incas of Peru, since the same causes tend to produce similar effects.

As well, when our democracies were created, especially between 1780 and 1880, the frequency of mandate renewal corresponded rather well to the nature of public affairs and existing communication links. Communities were fairly homogenous, lived on neighboring and relatively limited territories and problems were easier to solve. Between two and five years were enough to plan and carry out most policies; the absence of specialized tools to assess their results meant there was little inclination to adjust the aim in the meantime, except where it was generally agreed gross errors had been committed.

When colonial empires evolved, the need to maintain control over long distances compelled central authorities to either create forms of semi-autonomous governments (for example, the nomination of governors or viceroys to preside over councils of local dignitaries) or improve communication techniques. Thus England offered considerable rewards for the improvement of principal navigation tools (marine compass, reliable ship's clock) before the appearance of steamships, railways, telegraphs and radios. Unfortunately, the myopia and conservatism of certain elites forced the political systems of some countries to remain static, as though the world had stopped evolving with the sailboat and stagecoach. Only with Roosevelt and Kennedy did campaign politics begin to catch up with the electronic media; this wasn't the case for government politics. More important still, new technologies impose a degree of long-term planning that far exceeds the life span of most governments. The industrial success of states like Japan and South Korea demonstrates the advantages a stable regime can draw from a long-term planning system also able to adapt to changing circumstances rapidly. It's highly doubtful these countries would have achieved such results had they been submitted to electoral constraints like those found in North-American and European democracies; Korea was an authoritarian dictatorship and Japan, under the guise of an elective system, was run by an insular oligarchy controlling an irremovable party (in power for nearly 40 years without interruption) and an omnipotent public service.

Little is said by prominent authors about this aspect of political evolution; I believe the few examples mentioned above and minimal reflection will demonstrate that communication requirements have always been important in defining government structures, something that can only be accentuated henceforth, given the "information society" in which industrial states exist. In this context, electoral timetables dating from the 18th and 19th centuries often become virtual torture racks: the repercussions of major policies often arise only after a decade or more, so that a party must implement measures likely to benefit its successor (often its arch-rival). In return, the use of measuring and analytical instruments prompts short-term adjustments that can't be sanctioned by the electorate under the present system.

FOR OR AGAINST ALTERNATION

The classical doctrine assumes that alternation of power is good theoretically and practically. On the one hand, it perceives it as an indication of democratic health. On the other, as mentioned above in the discussion about political parties, this doctrine maintains that conservative and progressive groups take turns serving as deterrents and accelerators to structural and legal evolution; (from an economic perspective) the primitive capitalism of conservatives favors creation of wealth, whereas the social and humanitarian concerns of progressives help foster its equitable distribution. In both cases, time in opposition allows parties to recover from the wear and tear of power and revise their programs. But this only applies in certain conditions. The two main ones being a minimum of mutual trust and respect, and a genuine difference of view and proposed social blueprint. Nowadays, a prevalent animosity combined with mistrust prods each camp, on assuming power, to systematically destroy the other's work, rather than build on it.

In the past, left-wing parties were more ideological and inclined to a rhetoric of brutal change; but, once in power, they were compelled to spare the sensibilities of financial and industrial powers. This led them to dampen their excesses, to the extent their social measures were tempered by an awareness of economic constraints. For its part, the right-wing movement had a less trenchant discourse and was usually content with stopping or slowing down the movement without turning back the clock. However, Thatcherism and Reaganism prodded it to be much more dogmatic and intransigent; since the business world applauds the worst of its regressive policies, and since it ignores the alarms sounded by unions and other socially concerned groups, its conservatism becomes practically unfettered.

As a result, we've witnessed for a little over a decade ruthless privatizations, an undermining of social programs and anti-unionism. It's increasingly obvious, despite opposite claims by fanatic free-market economists, that this leads to a violent and potentially destructive counter-reaction from left-wing parties, if ever they assume power. In such a context of animosity and imbalance, alternation becomes dangerous and eliminates the possibility of long-term planning.

Exceptions to this rule are usually attributable to an absence of ideological parties; the alternatives are then purely election-minded groups (or incongruous coalitions) that lack definite policies and long-term plans, and whose sole ambition is survival. To this end, they seek out and conform to the electorate's lowest common denominator, regardless of the resulting incoherence. As a result, alternation has practically no effect ... and advantages of the brake-accelerator mechanism vanish. Long-term planning isn't threatened since it doesn't exist to begin with. On the other hand, short-term adjustments are guided neither by a vision nor by a clear perception of genuine social needs, but only by the marketing and propaganda concerns of re-election.

VISION AND PROPAGANDA

Political programs are increasingly based on opinion polls and studies, not on a coherent vision; often, the only difference between parties is tone and vocabulary. This raises numerous problems: a lack of internal logic, the absence of genuine alternatives, and a serious dearth of imagination and audacity in the solutions offered to unprecedented problems.

The electronic media is blamed for having too much influence on the electoral process. All it really does is reveal existing tendencies. By accelerating the pace of campaigns, intensifying tensions, highlighting incoherence, lies and mistakes, television creates nothing that didn't already exist in a less obvious form. The problem isn't the camera, but the process which makes it omnipotent; that process is an essential element of the democratic system.

The same applies to opinion polls and studies. Whether they influence the public matters little in the end, since the whole operation's purpose is to sway opinion by any possible means. It's difficult to imagine how a poll, even one that's been tampered with, could be more damaging than spiteful or mendacious propaganda ... However, although there's a growing consensus about the need to regulate polls, the least attempt to do the same with the statements of candidates immediately appears as an infringement on free speech. As a result, it's difficult for parties and politicians to clearly formulate and explain serious policies and trends, and just as difficult for electors to analyze them.

Parties and leaders are to a good degree elected on the faith of their promises, often made in eager emulation and purely as propaganda during the campaign; paradoxically, nothing in the democratic mechanism holds them to those promises once elected. On the contrary, ignoring pledges to the nation has become the rule rather than the exception. The only recourse is to defeat their authors in the next election. In the meantime, however, they may implement, without genuine opposition, policies that often correspond very little to the population's wishes, and which had been neither unveiled nor discussed previously.

DURATION OR TERM

Modern states elect their leaders for intervals that are pre-determined or roughly limited by custom. In antiquity (and recently still in various public and private organizations), this was done instead on the basis of a mandate or specific task whose duration varied. It would likely be interesting to re-examine such an approach, particularly in the case of a more or less pronounced return to participatory democracy: instead of electing leaders unconditionally for a given term, we might simply give them the "order" to carry out a specific and collectively-decided policy, and require them to account publicly for their success or difficulties at pre-determined intervals, that wouldn't necessarily be electoral.

We can imagine this method, which combines representation and direct democracy, might produce better results than the visibly inadequate system now in place. Whether this system holds democracy's ultimate salvation, as has been increasingly maintained over the last few years, is another matter.

– 8 –

THE FAILURE OF MODERNITY

One of the most astonishing and disquieting anomalies, for the rational individual, is the recent and noticeable return of superstition in the most advanced Western societies. This ranges from the most benign (or even socially useful) manifestations such as the renewal of religious sentiment, to the fanatical and sometimes murderous sectarianism for which the United States, in particular, has a knack—the Davidians of Waco, Texas were the most recent example. Between those extremes stand the "New Wave," alternative practices and various other forms of armchair occultism, belief in horoscopes and portents, even by public figures, and a tendency by some scientists to infuse spiritual "realities" into their very materialistic world views.

Relating the phenomenon is inadequate; deploring it even more so. Because it's neither an aberration nor a momentary folly, but a symptom. We must therefore stop treating its victims as lunatics or nitwits and inquire instead into the nature of their attitudes. In my opinion, it indicates a malaise of civilization caused by the failure of rationalism in the three forms most prevalent in the West: liberal humanism, democratic politics and scientific vision.

AN EXPLANATION THAT EXPLAINS NOTHING

Whatever Marxists may have claimed (and, after them, most social and political thinkers of the rationalist school), religion wasn't originally a device for social control. Unfortunately, political and economic leaders diverted it from its original purpose, which was to reassure man about an incomprehensible and threatening universe. Most primitive religions deified and thereby "explained" powerful and baffling natural phenomena: the sun, moon, tides, heaven, lightning, fire ... As soon as the nature of these manifestations was understood, religion became more abstract and social.

The perception of its original role accounts very well for periodic (notably over the last years) returns to religiosity and mysticism: when politics and science, which are supposed to explain and simplify life for the benefit of mankind, don't fulfill their promises, people revert to more primitive solutions. Moreover, since "official" churches have often made the mistake of dabbling into politics and trying to cohabit with science, they've opened the door to the most ancient superstitions (spiritualism, divination, horoscope) and sects. These groups pit their simplistic theories against complex scientific facts, and function mostly on the fringes of political parties, when not in direct opposition to them.

An important consequence of this evolution is that religions risk losing their social and political utility, which came from their ability to control the behavior of their faithful and make them more docile and passive; sects, which are often anarchic, don't fulfill this role as well as recognized churches, at least not until they've been taken over by the authorities (Christianity, for example). The notable exception to that rule is Islam, which maintains all its social importance and political utility; it has made no effort to adapt to the scientific view of the world, and usually abstains from co-optation by existing political powers, specifically by the fashionable trend of Western democracy. It's probably no coincidence that it's the only major religion still expanding today.

THE SCIENCE OF POLITICS

Since Auguste Comte, Proudhon, Marx and the Spencerians, science and politics have joined forces in promising to make life and the universe more comprehensible and hospitable. Moreover, political scientists have tried to transform the study of government systems and administration of power

112

into a precise science, as economists have done for their discipline. Similarly, political scientists pursue the double goal of analyzing political phenomena objectively and offering leaders advice and practical solutions to either govern more effectively, or simply stay in power. Machiavelli has had numerous descendants.

After a little over a century of this process, we must observe that if the first and theoretical aspect has evolved considerably, the second, which pertains to the application of the theory, hasn't nearly held its promises. The disorderly state of the world doesn't suggest that more "scientific" governments have made our lives simpler or more secure. For a time, they managed to create an illusion, notably (in the case of democracies) by blaming their difficulties and failures on "evil communists," while people's republics answered in kind by blaming "imperialist devils."

It's therefore likely the recent rise in political cynicism among Westerners, particularly their massive rejection of elites, is directly related to the collapse of communism: electors have had time to understand, at least nebulously, that the disappearance of an enemy blamed for all our problems has changed little in practice. Meanwhile, Eastern countries, some of which had brutally ousted their totalitarian leaders and demonstrated a touching but misplaced confidence in the ability of Western democracy to resolve for them difficulties it can't even settle for us, have begun to backtrack (Lithuania, Poland and Hungary).

If the Berlin Wall's collapse didn't usher in the "end of history" as a Japanese thinker has claimed, it at least represents a serious tear in the cloak of rationalism that had swathed politics. For example, the belief that democratic principles are immutable, but that politicians can obtain the results they seek within that framework and therefore hold their promises—even the most hare-brained—has been seriously shaken. More credit should be given to the opposing argument: ideals and structures can be modified, but once they've been adopted, they impose a logic and a dynamic that individuals and parties can only inflect minimally.

THE POLITICS OF SCIENCE

After viewing the universe mystically for most of its history, humanity briefly experienced generalized rationalism (at least in regions of the world that are allegedly "developed") which may have lasted from the eve of the first bourgeois revolutions to the last post-war period. This was a time when extraordinary progress in the physical sciences could convince us not only that nature was understandable, but that we were on the verge of acquiring a thorough understanding of it within the reach of any intelligent and informed individual. This conviction went as far as the pretentious claim that "nothing's left to be discovered," made by scientists at the end of the 19th century. It didn't last.

On the one hand, the average man has begun to see that reality is much more difficult to understand than previously thought: witness the atom, whose existence the Hiroshima bomb proved to the general public, the fabulous and burgeoning evolution of life sciences, the awesome size (and age) of the universe revealed by radio astronomy. On the other, if such an understanding is possible, it would be so complex and esoteric as to be limited to a few particularly powerful intellects. The adoption of abstruse and different jargons in each scientific discipline, which is perhaps inevitable, hasn't helped things.

Following that observation, it became easier, less frustrating and in many cases more effective to perceive the interaction between elements of our universe, at all levels, as random occurrences instead of the effects of a mechanism that is precise but too complex to be predictable. This path was chosen by many partisans of reason; their more numerous counterparts gradually allowed themselves to be seduced by a return (in various forms) to a mystical understanding of the universe, which at least had the merit of simplifying their lives. Once such a step is taken, it's very difficult to turn back. When vision becomes more a matter of faith—and therefore emotion—than intelligence, even repeated refutations lose their power to shake it.

HUMANIST GIANTISM

Liberal humanism is the third aspect of rationalism inherited from the Enlightenment. It claimed that society was perfectible through a measure of good will and the application of some universal principles. It promised a more peaceful, brotherly and humane world. Its goals were thought to have been reached on many occasions: following the two great "wars to end all wars" and more recently with the promises of a "new world order."

But that hope seems no closer than it was a few generations ago. The reasons for this probable failure are numerous:

a) Capitalism and the wealth it created allowed humanism to progress, but also created insurmountable obstacles to it, for example, by accentuating inequalities. North-South tensions are the best recent example.

b) The internationalist vision adopted by intellectuals never became widespread. Individuals continue to relate to local, regional or national communities, way before thinking of themselves as "citizens of the world." Moreover, the least pretext can once again reveal their mistrust, if not hatred, of all strangers.

c) The humanist tendency of denouncing unacceptable attitudes (nationalism, racism, religious sectarianism ...) without trying to understand or make allowances, doesn't eliminate them, but entrenches them more firmly though less perceptibly. Whenever given a chance, they reappear as violently and irrationally as in the past: for example, ethnic and religious dissension in the former USSR and Yugoslavia, racist movements in France and Germany.

All told, humanism has produced artificial, gigantic structures to which most people can't relate. Through ignorance or contempt, it has placed numerous local institutions in the hands of its adversaries. Since they are closer to the population, it therefore relates more readily to them. Here again, we must note a failure of rationalism.

THE SEDUCTIVENESS OF THE IRRATIONAL

The depth of this triple failure of rationalism may be questioned; it may be argued the extent of setbacks isn't as extensive for each of the three components. But this is unimportant; what matters is that the phenomenon is perceived as real and that it considerably increases the attractiveness of the irrational for many of our fellow citizens. This allure is based on numerous factors:

a) "Magic" formulas offer a reductionist view of the world that is much easier to understand, at least superficially, than the oversubtle, technical and abstract arguments of politicians, scientists and professional humanists.

b) These formulas provide metaphorical explanations which, at first sight, are simply verifiable in daily experience. Belief accepts all facts that confirm it and rejects or forgets those that refute it; this has a reinforcing effect which more rational approaches can't use.

c) Ultimately, according to Arthur C. Clarke's famous axiom, "any science advanced enough is perceived as magic." Modern technology is swarming with wonders that baffle the average individual; paradoxically, this increases faith in the miraculous instead of reducing it.

d) Emotional adherence to a simple religious or spiritual "principle" immediately eliminates the individual's feeling of powerlessness before the universe. Indeed, recourse to prayers, incantations or talismans, whatever their form, promises results no longer expected from the application of reason.

The revival of mysticism, even among allegedly enlightened Westerners, can only be a serious obstacle to the propagation of democracy, and even more to its critique and improvement. Mysticism is therefore of interest to us in that regard, although it's a subject that transcends the scope of this book.

- 9 -

A LACK OF ALTERNATIVES?

What alternatives do we have, if we reject democracy as a political system? The traditional answer is found in a famous typology used by most authors: governments by an individual, a group, or by all citizens, each system having two versions, one directed at the collective interest, the other to the benefit of those wielding power. However, we may ask whether this list includes all possible options, and especially whether recent evolution hasn't produced major changes that demand a new analysis. First, choices, even those within this scheme, are far from limited to a half-dozen, since each category has had multiple variations. As well, there are certain formulas that go beyond traditional alternatives, such as theocracy and dictatorship of the proletariat. Finally, the double pressure of modern complexity's requirements, and the tools offered by technology to solve them, strongly inclines us towards technocratic solutions that were unthinkable one or two generations ago. Therefore, before condemning our style of democracy outright, we must examine all these avenues and determine what latitude they allow us for developing a new formula that's acceptable in principle and in practice.

THE CLASSICAL DIVISION

The comparison used by Churchill, and referred to by most authors, is based on a definition of political structures that dates back to Herodotus, and which Aristotle systematized into a two-dimensional grid: in one direction are the number of people who share power, in the other, the way they use it. However, it has two drawbacks. First, it was conceived to

119

study the governments of small Greek city-states and applies imperfectly to larger modern entities. Second, it doesn't deal with some of the most important political principles devised over the last two centuries, particularly division of powers and the predominance of political parties. Although outmoded and incomplete, this grid is still often mentioned and it's a useful basis to assess various alternatives.

MONARCHY\TYRANNY

This is the system where power is exercised by one person, either in his own name or the community's. It's probably the most prolific political system in the history of mankind; perhaps even the most "natural" since it's usually the first to emerge in human communities. It takes on the current family structure based on paternal authority, and favors a strong central power, which is often necessary to ensure the protection of a community that's just been created, especially in a hostile environment.

Contrary to popular opinion and to recent practice, single leaders have often acceded to power through election, rather than overthrow or hereditary bequest. Community members agreed to name the most vigorous or astute individual among them as their leader. Traces of this process were found even in the hereditary monarchies of Europe: the election of the Western Emperor; Louis the Pious' naming his son, Lothair, as his successor by the "will of the people" as much as by the will of God. Monarchy became hereditary for three specific reasons:

a) The preservation of social peace and public security; the presence of an automatic method for choosing the next sovereign reduced the risk of conflict, which could go as far as civil war. The turbulent history of the succession of Roman emperors and the War of the Roses in England are good examples of this danger.

b) The definite advantage of systematically preparing a future leader to govern from early youth. In a subsistence economy, only a restricted number of community members can be released to fill positions that aren't directly productive. It's therefore important they be identified early and prepared for the tasks that await them.

c) The elite has a natural tendency of favoring its descendants and keeping "power in the family." This is often taken as the only motive; but, it's only played a secondary role, somewhat tipping the scales in favor of one formula over another.

In a monarchy, authority is defined by a rather explicit constitutional framework and succession is done in an orderly fashion, most often within the same family. In a dictatorship or tyranny, power is exercised without limitation (and is usually acquired by force). The classical typology distinguishes both types of individual power, according to whether they are used for the good of the community or that of its owners.

Numerous examples of both systems still exist. In practice, it isn't rare that one is exchanged for the other: a tyrant becomes sufficiently popular to create a legitimate hereditary dynasty, or a sovereign who obtained power rightfully begins to act like a despot and orchestrates an internal coup that releases him from constitutional constraints.

ARISTOCRACY\OLIGARCHY

This is government by a small clique; power is held by an insular group of citizens, either in their own name or the majority's. It assumes three principal forms that may combine in various ways. The first is the council of elders or Senate (in the original sense of the term), whose members are chosen on the basis of age and experience. The second is predicated on excellence, which explains its name as an aristocracy, a term that comes from ancient Greek and means "government by the best"; in its traditional form, it generally implies a division into hereditary castes, though this isn't essential, as is demonstrated by the modern version we call technocracy.

Finally, in a plutocracy wealth is the only criterion for membership in the ruling group.

The classical typology recognized only two of these forms: the aristocracy, which it identified as government by a minority, motivated by the public interest; and the oligarchy (a wider rendition of plutocracy), where the group holding power primarily benefits from its position and ensures its perpetuation. It's no wonder that prominent political analysts at the beginning of the century, like Weber and Michels, felt that democracy smacked of oligarchy!

DEMOCRACY\DEMAGOGY

In this system, the whole population holds power and exercises it either directly, or through its chosen representatives. In a bona-fide democracy, this is done with public interest in mind. If, on the contrary, there's an insistence on the rights and privileges of each voter, the classical theory holds this system to be a demagogy. Given this distinction, many of our modern democracies aren't what they pretend to be.

More specifically, Western-type democracies are divided into three principal categories: parliamentary, presidential and directorial. The third, only practised in Switzerland, is a peculiar survival of the French Revolution that runs counter to everything else; not only does it compel the executive (in theory at least) to be hardly more than a mere executant of the legislature's decisions but still, through referenda and "popular initiatives," it provides all citizens with a clearly more active role than is the case in ordinary representative systems.

The presidential system in its "pure" form has managed to take root practically only in the United States. It implies a president elected by universal suffrage who exercises executive authority with the help of a cabinet he appoints directly, that is completely separate from the legislature. Technically, he doesn't even have the right to introduce laws. The legislature is also elected by the people and acts as a check on the presidency, particularly by controlling its expenses (adoption of the budget) and reviewing nominations to important public-service positions. If the American system has survived, it's probably more due to custom than to some kind of constitutional magic. In many countries where it was tried, it quickly degenerated into dictatorship or shattered under the tensions between the two major branches of government.

The British-type parliamentary system is the most prevalent. Its legislature (at least its lower house) is elected, and an executive (cabinet) headed by a prime minister is chosen from its ranks. To govern, the executive must maintain the "confidence" of parliamentarians. In most cases, the legislative branch plays only a subordinate role, confirming decisions and adopting laws decreed by cabinet. This is mainly due to the influence of political parties, that impose a discipline that deprives their members of any initiative.

Some countries, like France, have adopted a hybrid formula that tries to reconcile the advantages of British-type systems with those of their American counterpart. Accordingly, they have executives accountable to legislatures and an elected president; depending on the extent to which the latter's powers are genuine, they tend to lean towards the presidential formula, without ever really attaining it. In any event, like all democratic systems save Switzerland's, they maintain a strongly oligarchic quality and sometimes have aristocratic affectations.

BEYOND TRADITION

The above grid, even revised and improved by modern authors, principally reflects the needs and ideas of antiquity. Historical evolution since then, and in regions of the world beyond the Mediterranean basin, reveals it doesn't nearly address all considerations. For example, what Greeks considered as political entities were tiny city-states whose populations didn't exceed half a million, and whose size was limited to the distance a man could travel on foot or horseback on a bad road in a single day. They didn't consider the specific problems of great empires; they knew about Persians and Egyptians but considered them to be "barbarians" whose political customs weren't particularly interesting (how can we blame them? Our own political scientists feel the same about Chinese or Arab empires).

Moreover, they hadn't discovered the division of power, and couldn't imagine authority might be split up and distributed among various institutions; their assemblies and courts were at once legislative and judiciary, and their executives entirely submitted to the people. Finally, since their philosophy placed the state above the individual, they didn't enjoy the benefits of a charter of rights and, being little inclined to religious sectarianism, hadn't conceived of the theocratic system save as an artifice of tyranny.

To get a better idea about available options, we must therefore add to the classic grid certain systems outside the usual categorization, examples of which are easily found in the modern world.

THEOCRACY

In this case, society is ruled not by laws adopted or decreed by governments, but by a code whose origins are allegedly divine and implemented either by civil administrators or a caste of priests. "Islamic republics" are the most striking examples of this system, though not the only ones. We forget that for centuries the Catholic church's principal ambition was to convert Europe into a theocracy where, according to the "two swords doctrine," kings and emperors governed only according to rules of the Gospel as interpreted by the Pope and bishops.

Two reasons that had little to do with political principles and individual freedoms thwarted that ambition: the emergence of nationalism, particularly in France and England, and the shattering of Christian doctrinal homogeneity, as a result of the Great Schism and the Protestant Reformation. Interestingly, two similar causes are preventing the emergence of a united "Islamic nation" (much more than the wisdom of our democratic thinking); namely, the religious sectarianism between Sunnites and Shiites, as well as ethnic and national differences between Arabs, Berbers, Iranians, Afghans, etc.

PEOPLE'S REPUBLIC

Communists invented the "class dictatorship" concept, which justifies the exercise of power—in principle temporary—by a single and strongly ideological party. The basic idea is simple: since bourgeois democracy is run by a restricted clique in the name of the dominant class, its influence can only be reversed by a similar system pointed in the opposite direction. Therefore, people's democracy consists of complete control by an authoritarian and quasi-military organization, which must act in the name and for the interests of the newly dominant working class. This structure will only disappear on the inevitable but distant advent of the classless society, with the "withering of the state."

The apparent effectiveness and coherence of this totalitarian approach have seduced numerous newly independent countries over the last decades, often with disastrous results. On the one hand, apparatchiks of the party that's "temporarily in power" tend to become permanent fixtures and give themselves numerous privileges; as a result, they quickly become the dominant class. On the other hand, wealthy bourgeois regimes that dominate the world economy have trouble accepting people's republics, if at all, and submit them to a kind of financial and political ostracism, forcing them to be in a "permanent state of war," as it were. This prevents any political evolution and further hardens the regime's authoritarianism.

Since the Berlin Wall's collapse and the USSR's demise at the end of the eighties, most people's republics have disintegrated. It's too early to tell whether they'll become democracies; the present climate certainly isn't conducive to optimism, since it's rather characterized by social and political disorders that, if we rely on all known precedents, are harbingers, if not catalysts of authoritarian dictatorships. Whether the United States can prevent this through military might is far from obvious, if what's happened in the former Yugoslavia since 1990 is any indication.

The most intriguing case, perhaps the most promising as well, is China, which has managed to maintain the soundness of its political system and launch a gradual conversion towards an original solution. The bloody Tiananmen incident, though a brutal triumph of the traditional reason of state over the individual, blinded most observers; through its decisiveness, Beijing probably avoided the kind of deleterious and extremely dangerous process we've seen at work in many other former socialist countries. China faces serious problems, but at least it's clearly preserved the political and social tools needed to confront them.

In the West, this evolution is interpreted as a move towards capitalism and democracy. However, a careful reading of information produced on this subject, in publications as conservative as "Time" and "Business Week," reveals instead the crystallization of a uniquely Chinese and hybrid formula. It preserves the principal elements of popular democracy and combines them with what it perceives as the most dynamic aspects of the Western free-market system; for example, new companies are partnerships between private capital, often provided by Chinese individuals living outside the country, and local or regional public institutions of a sociopolitical nature: townships, provinces, labor unions. Progress is achieved not by opening the country to everyone, but by decentralizing and liberalizing one region at a time, according to the nature and status of each local economy.

There is also good reason to think this isn't an innovation prompted by the collapse of world communism, but rather a consciously planned phase of a change launched nearly two decades ago. By 1987, "Scientific American" had already underlined that, in the previous decade, China had progressed from an almost chronic state of famine, to nutritional self-sufficiency, while the World Health Organization considered it the best-fed nation on earth. More impressive still, this leap forward was achieved with a 10% reduction in agricultural personnel; the equivalent of Germany's labor force was thereby made available either for industry or a more advanced education. It's difficult to perceive the recent surge of industrialization as pure coincidence ... it's easier to think that the recent and massive peasant migration towards cities, disorderly as it may be, is the result of a growth crisis rather than the indication of failure or fatigue.

THE CORPORATE STATE

This view was devised by economic thinker Peter Drucker who, over more than four decades, has analyzed major industrial and financial corporations and predicted their evolution. He, and especially some of his followers, have maintained that this authoritative and administrative structure could be advantageously adapted to the political realm. It somewhat inverts the reasoning of economic liberalism: rather than conferring maximal responsibilities to the private sector, governments should simply adapt business principles to their own operations. Some of their arguments have had practical repercussions, notably through the creation of crown corporations administered according to the usual rules of competition, and the adoption of internal accounting methods within ministries.

But Drucker himself now admits the general application of this approach creates as many problems as it solves. The first, which is purely practical, is that we see the system's defects and weaknesses much more clearly today than one or two generations ago: major corporations can become as fossilized and bureaucratized as government departments, if they're ever large enough and enjoy a relatively long period of prosperity. IBM, General Motors and a few others immediately spring to mind.

Second, the pyramidal and inegalitarian structure needed to make hard decisions directly contradicts any imaginable form of genuine democracy, and greatly resembles a military hierarchy. Promotions must be made according to merit and by co-optation throughout the organization, especially at the top; it's difficult to imagine how the "people's power" might be exercised in such a context, even in the very limited way it's done in representative democracies.

Finally, a functional relationship is difficult to establish between "management" and citizens. The latter, according to the corporate-state theory, would be both "employees" and shareholders of the system. How could they maintain a decision-making power at the highest levels—i.e., the "board of directors"—while taking orders from political executives and administrators in daily practice? This is the paradox confronting businesses controlled by workers; in a corporate state, the impact of this contradiction would be magnified since all spheres of life would be affected.

THE TECHNOCRATIC PROBLEM

Neither the ancients, nor the Enlightenment philosophers suspected the highly technical character that government activities would assume, as a result of industrialization and computerization. In their minds, public administration required no more competence than that of the educated and reasonably well-informed individual, having the outlook of a generalist. With today's extreme specialization in all disciplines, is electing "men of good will" as state leaders still adequate, or has technocracy in one form or another become, if not desirable, then inevitable even at the highest levels?

The choice of leaders was addressed in a previous chapter. It crops up again even more forcefully in the study of different political systems. Is it possible to reconcile technocratic demands with the democratic principle of "government by the people?" Or, is this a new and distinct system that imposes its own logic, mechanisms and structures, in direct conflict with concepts of election and representation?

Technocracy requires an elite (based on competence rather than blood or wealth) and a method of access to power that takes expertise into account. This expertise must be acquired formally through previous education, which implies that future leaders are selected and known in advance, and therefore not elected in the usual manner. They can't represent the people either, in the sense understood by democratic ideology: they don't lead because they are popular, but because they are competent.

Although we can imagine two approaches to technocracy that respect the "people's power" axiom, neither corresponds to the classical doctrine. The first is suggested by a practice borrowed from the private sector, but increasingly common in North-American municipalities: the executive is hired, not elected. He is, however, accountable to a representative assembly that essentially plays the role of a board of directors. The second is a formalization of the French system and recent American experiments: leaders aren't selected from a group of candidates; instead, "government teams" are chosen, consisting of experts who have had to prove their qualifications before a type of review committee resembling a senate.

Conclusion
BEYOND DEMOCRACY

L iberal democracy has fairly serious weaknesses of form and content. I feel I've adequately demonstrated it has the following theoretical and practical flaws: it doesn't allow for the selection of skilled leaders; adapts poorly to the planning required by a modern society based on knowledge and information; and leads to endless conflict within the community. We must add to this, shortcomings highlighted by other authors, particularly difficulties of application, and a cultural narrowness and myopia that make it a difficult-to-export product. Finally, democracy plays the same social role as the "principle of noble birth" did before its advent: it protects the status of a dominant class. Indeed, this indictment is now a commonplace. It's also deprecated today because it was Marxism's rallying cry for over a century ... but we forget it was taken up and systematically proven by numerous capitalist and liberal historians and political scientists. It must therefore be taken seriously. That the social group in power today bears the name of bourgeoisie or "middle class," rather than aristocracy, changes nothing ... especially since, after a loosening no doubt produced by the fear of communism, it now tends to tighten its ranks and return to a quasi-hereditary status and to "caste privilege" notions that are strongly reminiscent of its predecessors.

Can the system survive and expand despite all this? Probably, as long as American military and economic hegemony persists; the problem is knowing whether these flaws will imperil this hegemony, if they haven't already done so. What can we do to rectify the situation? The best I can offer, to avoid the facile accusation of purely destructive criticism, is to ascertain to what extent change is possible and what direction it might take. It will afterwards be up to others (or to myself) to suggest a certain number of leads that appear promising, either to redirect democracy along a less danger-ous and unequal path, or prepare a transition to a different system without the extreme violence that usually attends major political changes.

CAN WE AFFORD TO MAINTAIN THE STATUS QUO?

The first question that arises: why change? After all, this system seems to have led much of the West to a prosperity unequaled throughout history, provides comfort, security and an appreciable degree of freedom to the ordinary citizen, as well as the comfortable illusion of having a say in the way the world is run.

Even if that argument were essentially true (but only for a small number of nations), the system is nevertheless worn out, according to all observable signs. It has gone about as far as it can in the industrialized world and is starting to show serious cracks due to its internal contradictions and its inabil-ity to meet the demands of new circumstances. Moreover, it doesn't appear to have taken root durably in most other regions of the world. Wherever it did, it hasn't provided anticipated results in terms of the comfort and security of citizens and states.

The system is therefore obsolete. The four following points, mentioned earlier in other contexts, may convince any doubters. I believe it's important to highlight them since they're much more extensive and durable than minor incidents or economic fluctuations:

a) **The West's internal crises:** One secret of the West's economic and social success has long been that, while main-taining inequalities necessary to the dynamics of capitalism, it narrowed the gap between rich and poor. This paved the way to a more balanced, peaceful and secure society, even for the propertied classes. That tendency has been reversed and the gap has widened over the last decade, even in periods of prosperity and all the more during recessions. As a result, problems emerge that reduce the general quality of life (unemployment, vagrancy, drugs, crime, youth despair). Societal conflicts such as abortion and the environment sharply underline the increasingly tense and aggressive nature of our social surroundings and the absurdity of wanting to solve public interest problems on the sole basis of a confrontation between individual rights. Moreover, the visible disaffection with the "political class" in most so-called democratic countries threatens to drain the electoral mechanism of all significance, erasing democracy's last practical justification, since moral and philosophical ones have already been abandoned.

b) **The East-European time bomb**: The ostensible liberalization of former socialist republics is turning into a nightmare. Instead of providing the comfort, stability and security their citizens had dreamed of, democracy and capitalism have awakened the demons of ethnic hatreds and widened the gap between East and West, even in the most promising case, that of Germany's reunification. If a multitude of historical precedents is any indication, we can expect a decade or more of violent political change in that part of the world. A blood bath is very likely before the storm subsides in those countries—not a reassuring prospect, since some of them have global-range nuclear weapons! This may be the theatre most clearly demonstrating the danger and senselessness of wanting to "sell" our narrow view of the democratic ideal to other nations. They aren't ready for it, since they've never experienced it and certainly can't afford such a luxury given their state of turmoil.

c) **Islam and North-South relations**: The surge of Islamic fundamentalism has lasted long enough (about fifteen years) that it can no longer be mistaken for an accident. This movement has neither the support of intellectuals, nor that of the political and economic elites of the Muslim world. It also faces the combined efforts of Western powers; despite this, it relentlessly gains ground and undermines the democratic tendency (supported by all the above-mentioned powers) at nearly every encounter. Moreover, it's diametrically opposed to that trend at almost all levels; it's arbitrary, totalitarian, against technological progress and a rational view of the world, and offers poor protection for individual rights and freedoms. This is the best illustration (though far from the only one) of the impossibility of patching European ideas and systems over a culture completely foreign to them, if ever that culture was sturdy enough to withstand the first onslaught. This doesn't mean that fundamentalists are right, but underlines that their position, as absurd and regressive as it appears to us, appeals to enough people who are no crazier than we are, to triumph over what we believe to be the only possible truth. We must therefore admit either that this position has merits that escape us, or that our views are much less obvious than we believe.

d) **The rise of the Far East**: The only region of the world that has experienced explosive growth since the Second World War, which some observers feel to be disquieting, is the Asiatic side of the Pacific Rim. However, practically none of its countries have followed the democratic path to achieve this. On the contrary, all have emphasized collective responsibilities over individual rights, most have severely restricted freedom of speech, discriminated against minorities, planned their economies, limited access to their markets. It's only under pressure from their American invaders (Japan) or the effect of their new affluence, that some have adopted a more democratic facade; however, this is often only a mask that conceals oligarchic and dictatorial behavior. How much longer before developing countries realize the deception which the "Western model" is for them and conclude, as American economists have, that a reasonable but authoritarian dictatorship offers them a much better chance for success than the democracy we wish they'd practice?

PARTICIPATION OR DICTATORSHIP

With so many clouds gathering on the horizon, it seems logical that we desire and seek a change of course. But in what direction? I've devised, through a logical extension of the current evolution, four unequally probable answers.

The first is a renewal from within, in the shape, for example, of a "participatory democracy" as proposed by authors such as Canadian C.B MacPherson, and Quebecer Jacques T. Godbout. The idea is attractive in itself, but I can't imagine what mechanism would make it occur smoothly. To be achieved, it would require major structural modifications in existing political parties and organizations, as well as much greater citizen participation in public decisions. This practically means changing our representative system into an Athenian-style democracy, i.e., modifying the operating principle of our system, whose entire dynamic concentrates power in the hands of a narrow oligarchy and presupposes a high degree of citizen apathy.

Let's admit that participatory democracy rectifies much of the actual trend towards an adversarial society, by providing a "political" forum for debating controversial issues by other means than pressure-group confrontations; on the other hand, it only partially resolves planning and adjustment difficulties, while totally ignoring leadership-quality problems.

Finally, it presupposes that in favorable economic conditions, leaders who are unthreatened will yield some of their power under moderate and peaceful public pressure. This hardly seems possible, given the prolonged social and economic crisis now affecting us. Such a disruption would almost certainly be accompanied by violent jolts and a serious dislocation of the political system. However, this hypothesis is the only one that allows for the survival of democracy in a form that resembles the one we know.

The second possibility is that of a violent and perhaps bloody backlash, caused by the general exasperation of the working and middle classes, who have concluded their lot can only continue to worsen under the present system, as it has for a decade or more. This kind of danger is always rejected out-of-hand, but history teaches it may be much closer than we think. The French people never seemed so disorganized as on the eve of July 14, 1789; England never seemed more peaceful and prosperous than immediately preceding the 1642 Civil War. I don't want to be a harbinger of evil, but the possibility can't be discounted, given that all or most of the conditions needed for it seem to be present.

This entails two nearly inevitable corollaries. First, Russian events during 1991 show that a powerful military arsenal isn't very useful against a popular uprising in a country with liberal tendencies. From the first skirmishes, political leaders are reluctant to send in the troops; moreover, it isn't at all obvious those troops, most of whom are from modest backgrounds, wouldn't join the rioters. Some might protest things happened differently in the confrontation between Boris Yeltsin and the Parliament two years later; possibly, but who can still seriously claim the Russian president is acting like a liberal? Second, the toppling of a government perceived as weak and indecisive has usually occasioned, either immediately or following a brief period of disorder, the appearance of a "strong man" (Cromwell, Napoleon, perhaps Yeltsin?) who takes control autocratically. In other words, a violent replacement of elective systems would likely be followed by a series of dictatorships: farewell, democracy.

AN "INTELLECTUAL" SYSTEM

For the system to change, must we await the emergence of a new class which, according to Marxist theory, holds major power that doesn't have adequate representation within the political structure? Marx and his disciples thought the bourgeoisie would be the last of those classes and that the proletariat would replace it definitively; nowadays, it's clear that capitalism has managed, first to divide, then to recruit, a good part of the "working class" into its ranks. Moreover, the growth of automated machinery has greatly reduced the importance and strength of the latter, whose only weapon was its monopoly of labor. If there's to be a changing of the guard we must seek it along another path. But which one?

The answer most often given for nearly a generation, and which I'm tempted to espouse in this third hypothesis is that of the "intellectuals" in the most general sense, i.e., all those who work with their minds and control information tools. Why? Because the economy and the nature of commodities produced are changing before our eyes. In a world where the use of knowledge becomes increasingly important, those people begin to see themselves as the most able to govern ... exactly like members of the bourgeoisie did at the dawn of the industrial age. A certain logic is at work here: the Middle Ages and the Renaissance witnessed power shift from military leaders to great land owners; in the age of revolutions, it passed from the latter to the bourgeoisie, as the control of armed forces gave way to the management of land and then to the mastery of methods for the transformation of goods; with material production losing some of its importance to information processing, perhaps those who control this technique will decide to confirm their new dominance politically.

This transition may already be smoothly under way, beneath a cloak of classical capitalism. As financiers and brokers overtake manufacturers, we're witnessing a major shift in the significance of capital: money as an "information medium" is triumphing over money as a "production instrument." If banks and brokerage houses are taking on so much importance today, it's no longer because they're essential auxiliaries of industry, but rather because they exist, often without realizing it, in a new universe of knowledge management.

The political coincidence observed between the industrial leadership and the information-management class must not delude us. Although the replacement of one caste by another occurred brutally in some countries over two hundred years ago, this doesn't mean it must always be so. After all, such a transition befell England and Germany more gradually, while part of the gentry and seigniorial aristocracy subtly mutated into an industrial and commercial elite. Similarly, many great land owners from the preceding era were descendants of war-band leaders whom they replaced at the Renaissance. Nothing therefore prevents the bankers and technologists, who are at the vanguard of the next ruling group, to be sons of the bourgeois or nephews of industrialists or merchant barons as well.

Such a relatively smooth transition shouldn't blind us to the fact that these newcomers have neither the same objectives, nor the same views as their predecessors. The most likely consequence of the phenomenon must therefore be anticipated: liberal democracy, which is the bourgeoisie's mechanism of power, may very well be replaced by another system that's better adapted to our new masters, just like the feudal pyramid was supplanted by the centralized monarchy, which was in turn dethroned by the present system.

Should this happen, the "universal principles" we now hold so dear, will likely find themselves in the dustbin of history, along with the "two swords" doctrine and the "divine right of kings," which in their time had just as much importance and were felt to be as universal and absolute. For those whose curiosity is piqued by this, let's say the first theory mediated the conflict between temporal and religious powers in Medieval Europe; the second justified, through the "manifest will" of heaven, the hereditary succession of some families on most thrones of that continent a few centuries later.

A CULTURAL TRINKET

My last and most radical hypothesis: without significant modifications, liberal democracy's internal defects will continue to undermine and weaken Western societies until another region of the world takes the lead and in turn imposes its views. The Far East is the ideal candidate for that role, especially if Japan and China manage to surmount their thousand-year-old suspicions and find a common interest.

Whoever has studied those states, even superficially, is aware they are neither democratic nor liberal in their traditions or ways of thinking. Those that have adopted our system have most often done so as a facade and under compulsion.

What seems most likely is that once they've escaped current Western dominance, they would hastily revert to management methods more familiar to them and which correspond better to their mentality and culture. What form those systems take is a question I leave to the predictions of those more qualified than I. However, they wouldn't likely include ideas such as the primacy of individual happiness over collective interest, nor the equality of all citizens, regardless of their age, sex, ethnic origin or social status.

Accordingly, new masters may be tempted to spread their "ideal system" to the entire planet, as we've done over the last few decades, especially since some of those countries have a past that's earmarked by fierce imperialism. In such a case, Western-style democracy might not disappear, but it would become at best a quaint relic, a rather folkloric cultural trinket comparable to the courts of "kings who reign but don't govern" of old Europe or the facade of nomadic patriarchy maintained by current oil emirs.

AFTER US, THE DELUGE?

None of the hypotheses mentioned above seem either realistic or desirable to most of us. Yet, they're the only plausible ones, if we allow events to follow their course, the only ones publicly mentioned nowadays, along with a status quo whose long-term survival, as we've seen, is improbable. Is it possible to imagine another outcome, or must we, like Louis XV, see the coming storm and be powerless to avoid it: after us, the deluge?

I have no pre-conceived answer to that question, and wish to avoid the traps that have snared too many of my predecessors. The first pitfall is that we try to convince ourselves the situation isn't really as bad as we've imagined. The second:

we devise solutions that don't correspond to the problems we've exposed. Not only are the appropriate considerations numerous and complex, but they can't be quantified and classified in a well-organized framework. I'll therefore present them at random, in the hope others will be more successful at identifying an order and logic.

First, if there is a solution, it's to be found in a renewal of basic principles, not by modifying or repairing existing mechanisms and structures. The above-mentioned flaws are not due to circumstances, political personnel or technical difficulties; they are innate to the system. Democracy must be fundamentally questioned and reassessed. I believe we're at the threshold of a pivotal era comparable to the 6th century B.C. in China (Lâo Tse and Confucius) and Greece (appearance of city-states and philosophers), to the Hegira in Arabia and to the Enlightenment in Europe. That wasn't the time for half measures, nor is it now.

The debate must revolve around ideas. Not the pre-set ideas tossed back and forth like tennis balls every time the subject arises (participation, the role of citizens, individual rights, freedom of speech, etc.), but new ideas that run against the grain, and daring to the point of being considered eccentric, that address the very nature of the problem. Ideas with the strength and originality those of Plato, Locke, Montesquieu or Marx had in their day. We must not ask ourselves what type of democracy we want, but what type of system—without making arbitrary exclusions—can fulfill the genuine needs of human societies, both today and in the future.

Curiously enough, the old adage that "ideas rule the world" has now resumed much of its significance. In times of trouble and questioning, we almost inevitably turn to thinkers for guidance. I have felt such a tendency very acutely over the last few years. And the shift from a society based on the production and consumption of material goods to one dominated by information exchange, should favor a renewal of thinking and an increase in its influence. The world may be ready to be swayed by new ideas.

We must transcend the European and Western scale. Until now, we've had a penchant for sheltering our theories from any outside ideas or influences, under the pretext we "invented" political science. More than two thirds of the 180 or so countries at the UN aren't from the West; they include nearly three quarters of the world's population. On the one hand, our arrogance in excluding them from the debate is unbelievable; on the other, since some of those societies worked very well without our help for centuries, sometimes millennia, they'll likely make a valuable contribution to the debate.

We must not seek THE universal mechanism or formula, but rather principles likely to apply differently to various cultures and circumstances. Political systems are living organisms that evolve and have their own dynamic which must be respected, even while modifying or redirecting it. Little can be achieved by imposing a foreign system on a nation's institutions, without ascertaining how it adapts to cultural and religious traditions, to social and economic conditions, to needs and objectives.

Finally, devising a theoretical solution to the problem is inadequate. We must think, and very quickly, about how this solution translates into practice. Imagining utopias isn't difficult; determining how they can be realized without ending in blood bath or giving results opposite to those expected, is infinitely more complex. Supposing we do find a viable solution, certain areas of the world outside the West are beginning to feel an urgent need for it: Eastern Europe, most of Black Africa, the post-Gulf War Middle-East.

The future of mankind, especially that of Western civilization, may be linked to our own willingness and ability to accept that other nations redefine a political ideal that isn't simply a rather faithful copy of our own defective and threadbare system.

Montreal and Algiers
November 1992, September 1993

ANNOTATED BIBLIOGRAPHY

Hannah Arendt, *"The Origins of Totalitarianism,"* New York, 1951. A passionate and meticulous analysis. A history of totalitarian thought.

Aristotle, *"Politics,"* circa 325 B.C. The first systematic political science treatise; a development of Herodotus' grid. Questions the value of democracy as a leadership-selection method, but accepts the majority principle as necessary to guide the state.

Raymond Aron, *"Études politiques,"* Paris, 1972. A collection of essays and articles covering a rather lengthy period. Features views that are eclectic, yet very intellectual and French.

Bertrand Badie, *"L'État importé: l'occidentalisation de l'ordre politique,"* Paris, 1993. Despite the Western model's current success, it seems nearly impossible to export it to other cultures. According to the author, this is partly the fault of local elites, who haven't sought to make the necessary adaptations. A rigorous but dry treatise.

Pierre Bayle, *"Dictionnaire historique et critique,"* Paris, 1697. A rationalist approach, the first systematic defence of freedom of thought.

Jeremy Bentham, *"Political Sophisms,"* London, circa 1820. Critical and sometimes ironic aphorisms about politics by the creator of English utilitarianism.

Ibid., *"An Introduction to the Principles of Morals and Legislation,"* London, 1789. English utilitarianism's starting point. Opposed to notions of morality and right in politics; founds his entire system on utility, defined as the satisfaction of a need through the search for greater pleasure.

William Blackstone, *"Commentaries on the Laws of England,"* London, 1765. First critical compilation of a legal code essentially founded on custom (Common Law). This treatise has profoundly influenced lawyers throughout the West. Defends the notion that jurisprudence is the expression of the ancestral wisdom of nations.

Philippe Braud, *"Le suffrage universel contre la démocratie,"* Paris, 1980. A technical study of the universality of suffrage and its interpretation.

Edmund Burke, *"Reflections on the Revolution in France,"* London, 1790. A very critical assessment of the revolution by a conservative and bourgeois partisan of evolution. Institutions are respectable in themselves, since they incarnate the historical wisdom of nations.

Jacob Burkhardt, *"Force and Freedom,"* Zurich, 1871. A Swiss liberal thinker. Foretells the decadence of democracy through mediocrity.

Marcus Tullius Cicero, *"De Re Publica,"* 51 B.C. Believes there is a "natural" cycle for political systems that proceeds through monarchy, aristocracy, tyranny and democracy; a defence of the Roman Republic's mixed system.

Ibid., "De Legibus," 46 B.C. Description of natural law as the basis of positive law. One of the classical sources of 18th and 19th century liberalism and conservatism.

Auguste Comte, *"Plan des travaux scientifiques nécessaires pour réformer la société,"* Paris, 1822. An idealistic work of youth. The scientific creed of socio-political evolution and source of the positivism that would become a quasi-religion.

Marquis de Condorcet, *"Esquisse d'un tableau historique des progrès de l'esprit humain,"* Paris, 1794. Written in prison before the author was beheaded. A rationalist and encyclopaedist perspective. Displays an unshakeable faith in the constant progress of humanity.

Confucius, *"The Analects,"* circa 470, B.C. A collection of principles assembled by anonymous disciples following his death. Favours practical rules over grand theories; the purpose of government is the people's happiness rather than the ruler's greatness.

Christian Deschamps (editor), *"L'interrogation démocratique,"* Paris, 1987. Collective work from the Pompidou Centre; discusses various aspects of the democratic paradox. A multidisciplinary approach, juxtaposing the views of historians, political scientists, philosophers. Critical tone, a faint defence of principles that appear very shaky.

John Deverell & Greg Vezina, *"Democracy, Eh?"* Montreal-Toronto, 1993. By the same publisher as this book. A very critical analysis of Canadian democracy. Its only fault: the authors believe democracy works better elsewhere.

Denis Diderot, *"L'Encyclopédie,"* Paris, 1751. Achieved with the collaboration of most great thinkers of his time. An attempt to summarize all of mankind's knowledge. A liberal perspective and ferment of democracy.

The Economist, *"The Next 150 Years,"* London, 1993. A special issue of the respected British weekly attempting to predict the evolution of politics, science and economics over the next century and a half. Astonishingly thought provoking.

Moses I. Finley, *"Démocratie antique et démocratie moderne,"* Paris, 1976. A comparison of both forms of democracy that demonstrates the experience of antiquity remains relevant today. Emphasizes the relation (and distance) between leaders and the governed, and the conflict between individual freedom and public interest as well as the importance of popular consensus.

Jacques T. Godbout, *"La participation contre la démocratie,"* Montreal, 1983. A reflection on the contradictions between democratic ideals and the cooperative and participatory movement. The author is a sociologist and practitioner.

Ibid., *"La démocratie des usagers,"* Montreal, 1987. The social theory that underlies "La participation contre la démocratie."

Hammurabi, *"Code of Hammurabi,"* circa 1920 B.C. The first comprehensive codification of state laws. The precursor to the practical separation between the legislative and the executive.

James Harrington, *"Oceana,"* London, 1656. A utopian novel. The first one to relate the type of system to economic structures: one dominant proprietor: monarchy, some large proprietors: aristocracy, numerous smaller estates: democracy.

George W.F. Hegel, *"Philosophy of Right,"* Berlin, 1821. A philosophical view of history; features a nationalist approach and a dialectical system. Primacy of the state and society over the individual. Part of a comprehensive philosophical system that associates the rational with the real. Inspired Marx, Bismarck and the nazis!

Claude Adrien Helvétius, *"De l'esprit,"* Paris, 1758. A naturalist approach to the study of the human spirit. Everything emanates from the senses, abstractions don't exist. One of the starting points of the rationalist and secular spirit of the 18th century, close to Hume and utilitarianism.

Guy Hermet, *"Le peuple contre la démocratie,"* Paris, 1989. Are the people naturally democratic, or do they prefer "strong men"? An interesting theory that doesn't go far enough. A valuable source of recent bibliographical references.

Herodotus, *"The Histories,"* 435 B.C. The first attempt to write history outside the realm of legend. Source of the first classification of political systems according to the number of leaders: monarchy, oligarchy, demagogy.

Thomas Hobbes, *"Leviathan,"* Paris, 1651. Describes a totalitarian but reliable system. The first outline of the social contract concept, albeit outside the democratic context. Haunted by the insecurity and aggression of man against man. One of the starting points of modern political science.

Ibid., *"The Elements of Law, Natural and Politic,"* London, 1640. An attempt to base a legal system on natural law. Distinguishes between "natural" law, and "positive" or imposed law.

Paul Henri Thiry, Baron Holbach, *"Le système social,"* Paris, 1773. A moral view founded on rationalism; first hitch in the belief in "natural law." The writing is pedestrian but clear.

Thomas Jefferson, *"The Declaration of Independence,"* Philadelphia, 1776. The American republic's preamble; outlines democratic principles based on the pursuit of happiness. One of the founding charters of political liberalism.

Hans Kelsen, *"General Theory of Law and State,"* New York, 1961. Translation of a basic treatise concerning constitutional law. It dates from the beginning of the century and was used to draft several European constitutions, notably that of Austria. Rather technical.

Henri Laborit, *"L'Homme imaginant,"* Paris, 1975. Human evolution is mostly due, not to collective action or major policies, but to the creativity of individuals. Any doctrine that doesn't place imagination in positions of power (or at least allows it to flourish) will fossilize society.

Lâo-Tse, *"Tao-Te-Ching,"* circa 525 B.C. The "way of wisdom." A philosophical view of Chinese-style politics.

Philippe Lauvaux, *"Les grandes démocraties contemporaines,"* Paris, 1990. The political and legal structures of modern democracies. The first part contains a comprehensive discussion about political principles and the distinction between the rule of law, democracy and liberalism. Complicated and conventional, but of great interest.

Vincent Lemieux, *"Les sondages et la démocratie,"* Québec, 1988. A discussion about the nature of polls and their scientific dimension. A description of the process and its impact on politics from a Quebec perspective; its principles, however, are applicable anywhere.

Nicolai Lenin, *"Imperialism: The Highest Stage of Capitalism,"* Moscow, 1917. Capitalism can only survive if it leads to imperialism and to the systematic exploitation of colonial resources.

John Locke, *"Two Treatises of Government,"* London, 1690. The dawn of political liberalism. Advocates a constitutional monarchy. Clear style, confused structure.

John Lukacs, *"The End of the 21st Century and the End of the Modern Age,"* New York, 1993. According to Lukacs, a historian, nationalism has been the century's dominant force. The new barbarism in the East will endanger the "progress" imposed by the West.

Niccolo Machiavelli, *"The Prince,"* Florence, 1532. The first rigorous and even cynical analysis of personal power and the means for acquiring and maintaining it. One of the first books about politics that consciously strives to be objective.

Crawford B. MacPherson, *"The Life and Times of Liberal Democracy,"* Oxford, 1977. An assessment of liberal democracy's qualities and defects through a study of three historical models. Proposes a fourth model that is participatory. Idealistic.

Muhammad, *"The Koran,"* circa 634. Islam's Holy Book, it proposes a totalitarian system that combines the secular and religious. The free will presupposed by democracy contradicts Muslim fatalism, and the equality of citizens contradicts the respect it expresses for social classes.

Karl Marx, *"Das Kapital,"* London, 1867. A study of capitalism and the production of goods. A purely economic view of politics. The bible of scientific socialism.

Robert Michels, *"Political Parties,"* Berlin, 1911. A German classic from the beginning of the century, that exposes the "iron law of oligarchy," according to which the governing social class tends to perpetuate itself by any means and create an elitist "government club," even in democracies.

Montesquieu, *"L'Esprit des lois,"* Paris, 1748. An analysis of the relationship between the political system and the design of laws. Monumental but diffuse.

147

Thomas More, *"Utopia,"* London, 1516. Outlines an imaginary political system that is egalitarian and communist. An attempt to demonstrate the value of the democratic principle, in a non-liberal form.

José Ortega y Gasset, *"The Revolt of the Masses,"* Madrid, 1929. The class struggle pits not the proletariat against capital, but the people against the intelligentsia. An elitist perspective.

Robert Owen, *"Quest For a New Moral World,"* Glasgow, 1826. A moralist and collectivist approach to economic and social problems. A phase in the thought of the author-practitioner that has greatly evolved.

Thomas Paine, *"Common Sense,"* New York, 1776. A pamphlet on American independence having a utilitarian thrust. Many of its themes remain apropos.

Arthur Pigou, *"Economics of Welfare,"* London. Society must ensure the best prospects for the greatest number. A social view based on classical economic doctrines, of the Keynesian type.

Plato, *"The Republic,"* circa 390 B.C. A totalitarian view based on the communism of elites and civic education. Advocates a philosopher-king with no laws to check him. The work of his youth.

Ibid., *"The Laws,"* circa 340 B.C. Unfinished and posthumous. More moderate and less idealistic than the Republic. A blend of monarchy and democracy.

Marcel Prelot, *"Histoire des idées politiques,"* Paris, 1960. A history of ideas according to themes, with emphasis on classical authors. Completes the book with the same title by Touchard and that of Sabine.

Joseph Proudhon, *"Qu'est-ce que la propriété?"* Paris, 1840. Source of the expression "property is theft."

Ibid., *"Solution du problème social,"* Paris, 1848. The most representative expression of socialist thought before Marxism. Features mutualist views that survived until recently in French trade-unionism.

Stephen Rials, *"Textes constitutionnels étrangers,"* Paris, 1991. A compilation of constitutions from many countries, including the United Kingdom, United States, Switzerland, Spain, Germany. Emphasizes civil liberties and rights of man.

Jean-Jacques Rousseau, *"Le Contrat social,"* Paris, 1762. Massive and somewhat confused. Man is good, society corrupts him. A return to the state of nature or to a notion of the "minimal" state that will be taken up by 19th century English liberals. Features the "general will" which underpins the classical French definition of democracy.

George H. Sabine, *"A History of Political Theory,"* New York, 1971. A commentary on the evolution of political ideologies. Thorough and fascinating, contains opinions that are often critical. Complements Touchard. A good study of the socio-economic context surrounding the evolution of political ideas.

Claude-Henri de Saint-Simon, *"Réorganisation de la société européenne,"* Paris, 1814. A description of saint-simonism, a politico-economic doctrine that played an important role in France throughout the 19th century and particularly during the Second Empire.

Joseph Schumpeter, "Capitalism, Socialism and Democracy," Harvard, 1942. A description of the confrontation between the century's two dominant systems and their internal contradictions. Predicts the end of capitalism and its replacement by socialism. A penetrating analysis of liberal democracy equivalent to a demystification.

Oswald Spengler, *"The Decline of the West,"* Berlin, 1917. An original hypothesis based on the notion that a culture's decline begins when it becomes a civilization. Very influential in Germany between the two wars; anti-Marxist, but adopts the Hegelian idea concerning the inevitability of historic phenomena.

John Stuart Mill, *"Considerations on Representative Government,"* London, 1861. A proposal for reforming English democracy highlighting universal suffrage.

Ibid., *"On Liberty,"* London, 1862. Posits individual freedom as a fundamental and almost unique principle of political philosophy. The only exception to the rule being "protection of the self."

Ibid., *"Principles of Political Economy,"* London, 1848. A description of the classical liberal economic doctrine. Influenced by Bentham and utilitarianism. Close to Ricardo; a bourgeois view that is parallel but opposed to Marx's proletarian perspective.

Ibid., *"Utilitarianism,"* London, 1861. A critical development of Jeremy Bentham's theories. A classical description of that ideology.

Sun Yat-sen, *"The three principles of the people,"* Peking, 1923. An elitist liberal perspective grafted to another culture. Metaphor of the people, the limousine and the driver.

Richard Henry Tawney, *"Religion and the Rise of Capitalism,"* London, 1926. Establishes the link between Protestant egocentrism and the egotism of the classical-liberal economy. Demonstrates, with Weber, that capitalism and democracy are cultural phenomena arising from European Protestantism.

John Clayton Thomas, *"The Decline in Ideology in Western Political Parties,"* Beverly Hills, 1974. Discusses the neutralization of political differences between parties in Western democracies; this reduces the possibility that new ideas will emerge.

Alexis de Tocqueville, *"La Démocracie en Amérique,"* Paris, 1836. An admiring description of the political structures invented by Americans. Expresses a fear that democracy will fail as a result of the mediocrity of the leaders it produces.

Jean Touchard, *"Histoire des idées politiques,"* Paris, 1973. A very detailed history, containing an abundant and critical international bibliography. The tone is more objective than that of Sabine, though the description is less clear. A very French perspective.

Max Weber, *"The Protestant Ethic and the Spirit of Capitalism,"* Berlin, 1904. A sociological analysis of capitalism. Strongly suggests that liberal democracy is a "cultural" product that is specific and difficult to export.

Xenophon (pseudo), *"The Constitution of Athens," circa 425 B.C. An early aristocratic critique of democracy.*